THE LAST HOUR

STUDY GUIDE

STUDY GUIDE

THE LAST HOUR

AN ISRAELI INSIDER LOOKS AT THE END TIMES

AMIR TSARFATI

Chosen
a division of Baker Publishing Group
Minneapolis, Minnesota

© 2023 by Amir Tsarfati

Published by Chosen Books
Minneapolis, Minnesota
www.chosenbooks.com

Chosen Books is a division of
Baker Publishing Group, Grand Rapids, Michigan

Printed in the United States of America

ISBN 978-0-8007-6326-8 (paper)
ISBN 978-1-4934-4108-2 (ebook)

Cover design by Rob Williams, InsideOut Creative Arts, Inc.

Baker Publishing Group publications use paper produced from sustainable forestry practices and post-consumer waste whenever possible.

23 24 25 26 27 28 29   7 6 5 4 3 2 1

CONTENTS

SYNOPSIS OF THE LAST HOUR

Looking at the Long, Winding Road of Prophecy

In his book *The Last Hour*, native Israeli believer Amir Tsarfati weaves his testimony with the prophetic Word of God to help others find that same gift of eternal life.

This study guide supplements the book and will help you search the Scriptures for the truths presented in each chapter of *The Last Hour*. You will . . .

- Read the Scriptures to mine each truth so needed by the world today.
- Gain an overview of Israel, the nations, the Rapture, the man of lawlessness and the Days of Ezekiel.
- Learn practical application by gaining a knowledge of the truth and wisdom the prophetic Scriptures offer to man.
- Develop a deeper knowledge of your God and Savior by interacting with the Scripture as well as see the hope the believer has in the midst of chaos.

The book and study guide have been written to "wake up the Church, to warn nonbelievers and to speak of the blessed hope that believers have" (*The Last Hour*, page 28). Get ready for your journey!

1

LOOKING BACK BEFORE
LOOKING FORWARD

I once heard a man say that it is important to let people know where you sit before you tell them where you stand. To that end, I believe it is necessary for you to know who I am prior to reading what I believe. God has led me on a unique journey that has made me the man I am and contributed to how I view His Word.

The Last Hour, pages 18–19

I n the introduction to his book, Amir tells us where he lives—in the Galilee area of Israel. He can view the Valley of Megiddo from his front porch. He lives where battles have taken place and where armies will assemble for the last battle over Jerusalem. He is from the tribe of Judah. He was in the Israeli Defense Force and served in Jericho at the time it was to be turned over to the rule of the Palestinians. The Valley of Megiddo and Jericho are prominent places in the Bible, and the tribe of Judah has great significance concerning the Messiah.

The Tribe of Judah

Read Genesis 29:21–35.

What do you learn about Judah from this passage?

About Judah's mother?

About Judah's birth order?

About Judah's father?

About the meaning of his name?

Genesis 38 tells the story that connects Judah's tribe to the genealogy of Jesus. He was the father of the twins, Perez and Zerah, by his daughter-in-law Tamar. Perez and his and father are found in Jesus' genealogy in Matthew 1:2–3.

Judah made an unwise, sinful choice at that point in his life, but God gave him grace and a prophecy at the end of his father Jacob's life.

Read Genesis 49:8–10. What prophecies are given to the tribe of Judah?

Verse 8

Verse 9

Verse 10

Jacob was told that the kingship in Israel was to come from the tribe of Judah *until* Shiloh comes—a reference to "the One whose right it is," the meaning of Shiloh.

Now to you, O profane, wicked prince of Israel, whose day has come, whose iniquity shall end, thus says the Lord GOD: "Remove the turban, and take off the crown; nothing shall remain the same. Exalt the humble, and humble the exalted. Overthrown, overthrown, I will make it overthrown! It shall be no longer, *until He comes whose right it is*, and I will give it to Him."

Ezekiel 21:25–27, emphasis added

There have been those in the past who were overthrown by God, false rulers. The Holy Spirit is leading Israel and us to the feet of the Messiah, whose right it is—He is the Lion from the tribe of Judah!

For the children of Israel shall abide many days without king or prince, without sacrifice or sacred pillar, without ephod or teraphim. Afterward the children of Israel shall return and seek the LORD their God and David their king. They shall fear the LORD and His goodness in the latter days.

Hosea 3:4–5

Is this the state of Israel today?

What is the promise stated that is yet to be fulfilled?

Today, Israel and the world are in need of the One whose right it is to rule from the throne of David—Jesus Christ, the Messiah of Israel. They are without a king or prince or priesthood because they have rejected the One whose right it is, but Hosea tells us that in the future, Israel will return and seek Him and recognize Him as their rightful King, the Lion from the tribe of Judah! We all need to seek Him and recognize Him as our rightful King today!

Read Genesis 43:8–9. What did Judah promise his father he would be for his brother Benjamin?

Whose future action did that prefigure? How?

King David was from the tribe of Judah, as were all the kings of Judah until the Babylonian captivity. Israel had no kings from the time of the Babylonian captivity until Jesus, the King of kings, came in the fullness of time as the Messiah of Israel, the Son of David, from the tribe of Judah (see Luke 3:30–31), perfectly fulfilling all prophecy concerning the Messiah.

- Jesus is ruler of the _____ of the earth (Revelation 1:5).
- Jesus is the _____ from the tribe of Judah, the Root of _____, who has overcome so as to open the book and its seven seals (Revelation 5:5).
- Jesus is coming as the reigning _____ of kings and Lord of _____ (Revelation 19:16).
- He is the Root and descendant of _____, the Bright and Morning Star (Revelation 22:16)!

This is the Messiah, from the tribe of Judah, who came to save us from our sins and who is coming again to fulfill all prophecy and to set up His Kingdom on earth. It is very special that many Jews have passed on to their children the name of their ancestral tribe. Amir has been blessed to know his ancestry.

Jesus is our blessed HOPE!

What are you thankful for today? Write out your prayer of thanksgiving to the King of kings.

Jericho

Jericho is a modern city today that was turned over to the Palestine Liberation Organization so that local Arabs could govern themselves as a "state to be"—a part of the Oslo Accords signed in 1993.

A brief overview of Jericho:

- Joshua fought the battle of Jericho when the second-generation sons of Israel first entered the land of Canaan (see Joshua 6).
- It is located ten miles northwest of the Dead Sea and seventeen miles from Jerusalem.
- It is called the City of Palms (see Deuteronomy 34:3).
- In the New Testament, Jericho is mentioned in the parable of the good Samaritan (see Luke 10:30).
- It is still a thriving city today, but the first city in Israel ever to be placed under Arab control.

Read Joshua 6:25. Who was saved as a result of the Israelite victory over Jericho?

Is she of significance to the genealogy of the Messiah? Hint: See Matthew 1:5.

Read Joshua 6:24–26. What was the instruction of Joshua concerning the city of Jericho after it was burned and the consequence for not following the instruction?

Read 1 Kings 16:34. Who disregarded the instruction of Joshua (equated with the Word of God in this passage) not to rebuild the city of Jericho? What happened?

Jericho stands today and was a part of Amir's life. He notes in the book that Jericho is where he began to fall in love with the "idea of leading people into the beauty, wonder and truth that are found" in his country, Israel (*The Last Hour*, page 27).

The Valley of Megiddo

Amir states, "It is hard to get the end times out of your mind when [the Valley of Megiddo] is staring you in the face each day with your morning cup of coffee" (*The Last Hour*, page 17).

The Valley of Megiddo is part of the Valley of Jezreel in northern Israel.

- Mount Megiddo today is a hill overlooking the large valley where the current kibbutz is located.
- It is where Deborah and Barak fought a battle (see Judges 4).
- It is the area where the deaths of Ahab and Jezebel occurred.
- It is where King Saul and King Josiah died.
- The Megiddo of King David's time already had fifteen layers of destroyed cities beneath it.
- Napoleon believed it to be the perfect location for a battle.
- It was an ancient trade route between the Jordan Valley and the coastal plain, also known as Esdraelon.
- It has been identified as the site of the gathering of the armies of the world before advancing on the final battle for Jerusalem; it is also known as Har-Magedon, Mount Megiddo (see Revelation 16:16), or Armageddon in English.

Read Judges 4. Who sold Israel into the hand of Jabin, king of Canaan (vv. 1–2)?

What did King Jabin have, and how long had he oppressed Israel (v. 3)?

Deborah told Barak to go to Mount Tabor with men from which two tribes (v. 6)?

The Lord had told Deborah He would draw the commander of the army and his chariots out, and the Lord would sell Sisera into the hands of a woman (vv. 7–9).

Describe how the victory came for Israel (vv. 11–16).

Describe how Sisera was defeated (vv. 17–23).

Revelation 16:12–16 describes the final gathering of the kings of the whole world at Mount Megiddo in the Jezreel Valley, where Sisera was drawn by the Lord centuries before. Revelation 19:19 says the armies and the kings of the earth will gather together to make war against Jesus Christ and His army. Once again the Lord Jesus will fight for His people and they will be victorious. This time the armies will gather there to march to Jerusalem to annihilate the nation of Israel. Instead, those very armies will become a feast for the birds (see Revelation 19:21) because they are no match for the One on the white horse from heaven!

Read the Song of Deborah and Barak in Judges 5. Verses 4–5 describe what happened in Israel in the days of Deborah and Barak. They foreshadow Jesus' coming from Seir and Edom in that final battle. Can you see any similarities?

Read Isaiah 63:1–6. Try to identify similarities between that description and the description in Revelation 19:11–21.

These are the end times that are prophesied and warned about throughout the Bible, in both Old and New Testaments. These events are studied in The Last Hour. This book and study guide have been written with a passion to "wake up the Church" in the last hour, to "warn nonbelievers and to speak of the blessed hope that believers have" (The Last Hour, page 28).

2

GOD WANTS YOU TO KNOW HIS PLANS

Two millennia later, when we pick up our Bibles, we hold in our hands exactly what God determined we would need to know about Him, about creation and about our past, present and future. It is all there for us to read, learn and understand.

The Last Hour, page 42

The quote from the book shows us exactly what we need to know about the Bibles we have today. They are preserved miraculously by the almighty God, possessor of heaven and earth. If He is who He says He is, the Creator of everything, then He is more than able to preserve His written Word for us.

This study session will concentrate on some truths learned in chapter 2 that we can glean from the Bible.

1. God wants to be known.
2. God is the Author of absolute Truth.
3. Prophecy is in the Bible from Genesis to Revelation.
4. Knowledge brings peace; confusion brings weakness.

A God Who Wants to Be Known

The apostle Paul tells us in Romans 1:19–20 that God wants to be known. List three things from this passage God wants us to know about Him.

1. _____

_____

2. _____

_____

3. _____

_____

What invisible attribute(s) of the Creator God does creation help you see or know?

What does creation show you about God's eternal power?

What does creation show you about the Godhead?

Romans 2:14–15 says that Gentiles who do not have the law by nature do what is in the law because their conscience lets them know what is lawless and what is lawful. How would you explain that concept to another person?

Creation is not the only way God has revealed Himself. He spoke to and through the prophets. Isaiah is one of those prophets who wrote down exactly what God, through the Holy Spirit, inspired him to write.

Read Isaiah 45:18–19. List at least four things God says about Himself in this passage that are absolute truths about God.

1. _____

_____

2. _____

_____

3. _____

_____

4. _____

_____

- Daniel 2:28 says, "There is a God in heaven who reveals secrets, and He has made known to King Nebuchadnezzar what will be in the _____ _____."

This passage tells us that God wanted a Gentile king to know what would be taking place in the future from the time of that king's rule in 605 BC until the coming of the Messiah's Kingdom. Our God is the one who knows the end from the beginning, and He wants us to know His plan of redemption for us! That is awesome!

Here is further application for us to take away from this event in Daniel with a Gentile king:

- God wanted Nebuchadnezzar to know the future, even though Nebuchadnezzar was going to pass from the scene and other world kingdoms would come and go. He was told there is a God in heaven who is in control of all kingdoms of the world and it was not Nebuchadnezzar.
- God used His Jewish prophet, Daniel, to explain this mysterious dream of Nebuchadnezzar's concerning the future of the world—not a Gentile prophet.
- In Daniel 2:47, Nebuchadnezzar stated that Daniel's God is "the God of gods, the Lord of _____, and a revealer of secrets."
- Daniel was promoted as well as the three Jewish boys, Shadrach, Meshach and Abednego.
- This prophecy did what all prophecy should do for all of us—it changed Nebuchadnezzar's mind about the God of Israel and the nation of Israel, and ultimately, by Daniel 4, it brought him to a saving faith! That is the ultimate application!

The Truth about Absolute Truth

Jehovah in the Old Testament is the God of Truth. Jesus came, and He is the truth, the way and the life. List what these passages teach us about the God of all truth and His Word:

Psalm 31:5

Psalm 33:4–5

Psalm 43:3

Psalm 57:10; 61:7; 69:13
What two attributes of God are listed?

Psalm 85:7–11

Psalm 96:13
What is He coming to do, and how?

Psalm 108:4

Psalm 115:1
Why does He receive glory?

Jeremiah 7:28
What is the warning to Judah about truth?

Zechariah 8:3

What are the truths in this prophecy of the Second Coming?

Zechariah 8:16–17

What is the emphasis in this passage?

John 14:6

Who is truth?

Since you have purified your souls in obeying the truth through the Spirit in sincere love of the brethren, love one another fervently with a pure heart, having been born again, not of corruptible seed but incorruptible, through the word of God which lives and abides forever.

1 Peter 1:22–23

How does Peter say we purify our souls?

How are we born again, according to Peter?

Our God is Truth. Thus, all Truth begins with Him and is based on Him. He gave us the Bible so that we could know the Truth—at least as much as He saw fit to share with us. We can know the Truth about His creation of all things. We can know the Truth about sin and His sacrificial provision for our salvation. We can know the Truth about the meaning of life and our purpose on this planet. And, yes, we can know the prophetic Truth about God's plans for the future of this world.

The Last Hour, page 36

Prophecy Is Biblical

Second Timothy 3:16–17 gives a list of what Scripture is given by God for:

1. _____

2. _____

3. _____

4. _____

5. _____

"All Scripture" in that verse includes the 25 percent of the Bible that is called prophecy. Without it we would have an incomplete understanding of the complete plan of God—the God who knows the end from the beginning and has shared that plan in His Word. We certainly would not know how things will end or what our own destinies will be.

The first prophecy in the Bible is found in Genesis 3:14–15:

The LORD God said to the serpent: "Because you have done this, you are cursed more than all cattle, and more than every beast of the field; on your belly you shall go, and you shall eat dust all the days of your life. And I will put enmity between you and the woman, and between your seed and her Seed; He shall bruise your head, and you shall bruise His heel."

Galatians 3:16 says, "Now to Abraham and his Seed were the promises made. He does not say, 'And to seeds,' as of many, but as of one, 'And to your Seed,' who is Christ."

The Genesis prophecy was spoken to the serpent in the Garden of Eden, letting Adam and Eve and the serpent know that God was in control of the destiny of the serpent and the destiny of the descendants of the woman Eve and mankind. This first prophecy set His plan in motion to redeem mankind through the Seed of the woman, the God-Man who would die as the ultimate substitute in mankind's place so that man could rule and reign with Him on earth as was originally intended. The rest of the Bible is the unfolding story of redemption. Jesus Christ (Messiah) is the Seed of woman prophesied all through the Old Testament—the One who would have a miraculous birth!

Let's look at a few key prophecies of the Messiah and our future:

Micah 5:2 says the Messiah would be born in _____. What indicates His eternality in this verse?

In Isaiah 53, what is prophesied?

In Psalm 110, Jehovah is speaking to David's Lord, the Messiah. What is the prophecy?

What is the prophecy in Daniel 7:13–14 detailing?

In Matthew 24:30–31, Jesus is referring to the Daniel prophecy that He will fulfill in the future when He returns. What will He do? How?

Read Revelation 19:11–16. What is being described in this passage?

Revelation 20:1–3 describes the destiny of Satan. What is it?

In Revelation 20:15, what is the destiny of those whose names are not written in the Book of Life?

Revelation 22 describes your destiny if your name is written in the Book of Life of the Lamb. What do you as a believer have to look forward to?

Knowledge Brings Peace; Confusion Brings Weakness

Read John 14:27.
What does Jesus promise?

We must believe His Word to have that peace and knowledge only He brings to us.
What truths in the following Scriptures bring you peace?

John 14:1–2

John 14:16–18

John 14:29

John 16:7, 13

Application Truths from This Session

1. God is the God of peace and truth, not confusion (see 1 Corinthians 14:33).

2. The prophecies of Jesus' first coming were given from 1,000 BC to 400 BC and were all fulfilled exactly as prophesied.

3. We can know that all the prophecies given by Jesus and the Old Testament prophets about His Second Coming will be fulfilled exactly as prophesied because God's Word never returns void (see Isaiah 55:11).

4. John 16:33 is a promise of Jesus spoken to His disciples but is true for us as well. Write it out and commit it to memory.

5. Our promised future is to live in the City of Truth with our Prince of Peace. We hold fast to these and all biblical truths.

6. The Scripture passages listed in this lesson and others can be copied in a journal for you to refer to when the "author of confusion"—the enemy—tries to steal from you the peace that passes all understanding.

7. You might begin to reflect on other Scriptures as well that bring you hope and comfort and add them to your journal. The Word is living and alive and will bring you peace and comfort! Shalom!

3

UNDERSTANDING PROPHECY:
TWO-BY-TWO

When a prophet prophesies, one of two things may be happening: He or she may either be *forthtelling* a message of God or *foretelling* the plans of God.

The Last Hour, page 43

This study will look at Scriptures that are a prophetic forthtelling of a message and other Scriptures that deal with foretelling the future of Israel and the world.

Prophets of Israel Who Brought Messages of Condemnation and Warning

The prophets of Israel were told to go to the people at various times in their history and declare to them

- Condemnation of their sinful actions
- Commands to change, which will bring a solution to their dilemma
- Warning of consequences if no change

Jeremiah and Ezekiel were contemporaries. Jeremiah lived in Jerusalem, and Ezekiel was taken in the second siege of Jerusalem to live in Babylon at the time Daniel the prophet was in Babylon. All three men prophesied messages of warning and foretelling of the future as well. Their messages were for their time as well as for our time, so we will be looking for fulfillment then and in the future, as well as application for us.

Jeremiah, the forthteller

Read Jeremiah 4:1–4. Look for the reasons God is asking for a change of behavior.

List the specific things Jeremiah tells Israel to do:

Read Jeremiah 4:6–9. Where is great destruction coming from?

Jeremiah 4:10–18 gives more reasons for this coming destruction. List them below.

This was the condition of the nation of Israel right before 605 BC, when Nebuchadnezzar came and took the first group, including the teenager Daniel, captive to Babylon. He invaded again in 597 BC and 586 BC, taking two more groups captive and burning the Temple.

What can you learn about God from Jeremiah 4 and the seriousness of obedience to His Word? List those attitudes below and take time to examine your heart for those same attitudes and actions. Confess your shortcomings and ask for the power of the Holy Spirit to live out a godly life to the glory of Jesus!

Ezekiel, a foreteller

Ezekiel was taken captive in 597 BC and wrote his prophetic book from Babylon. He gave many forthtelling messages to the captives expecting action from the people, but he gave many prophetic messages foretelling the future of Israel and specific countries in relation to Israel. Let's look at the message in Ezekiel 12:

- God the Lord told Ezekiel he lived among a _____ house (vv. 1–2).
- He was to prepare to go into _____ —though Ezekiel himself was not rebellious (vv. 3–4).
- Captivity would be in the land of _____ (v. 13).
- Name a result that would come from the scattering (v. 15):

31

- What is the promise, and what are the two reasons for it (v. 16)?

- What were the people saying about the true prophets (vv. 22–23)?

- What were the people saying about Ezekiel's vision (v. 27)?

- God has the final word! What did the Lord God say to tell them (v. 28)?

There were mockers and scoffers in Ezekiel's day as there are today. The important lesson for us today: Do we listen to the Word of God and believe its warnings and messages, or do we ignore it? What is your response to the Word of the Living God?

Jonah, a forthteller on the regional track

Jonah is a prophet on the regional track—sent to prophesy to a Gentile nation!

- "Arise, go to _____, that great city, and cry out against it; for their _____ has come up before Me" (Jonah 1:2).
- "Jonah arose to flee to Tarshish from the _____ of the _____" (1:3).
- "But the LORD sent out a great _____ on the sea, and there was a mighty tempest on the sea, so that the ship was about to be broken up" (1:4).
- The men realized the calamity had struck because of someone on the ship; they cast lots and the lot fell on Jonah (see 1:5–7).
- When asked where he was from, he admitted he was a _____ who feared the Lord, "the God of heaven, who made the _____ and the dry _____" (1:9)!
- They asked Jonah what could be done to calm the sea, and he said to throw him in the sea—he recognized the tempest was because he was running from the Lord (see 1:11).
- The men prayed to be absolved of innocent blood, threw Jonah into the sea, offered a sacrifice to the Lord and made vows because they _____ the Lord greatly (1:14–16).
- The Lord appointed a great _____ to swallow Jonah—for how long (1:17)?

- Jonah understood he had been banished from the sight of the Lord in the belly of the fish, yet he appealed to Him for His mercy (see 2:4).
- Jonah 3:4 records the concise message Jonah was to "foretell." Write the message:

- What is the response of the people to the message (3:5)?

- What is the response of the king of Nineveh (3:6–7)?

- What is God's response to Nineveh (3:10)?

- What is Jonah's reaction to the response of Nineveh (4:1)?

- The Lord God appointed a plant to shade Jonah, who was still unhappy; then God appointed a _____ to attack the plant and prepared a scorching _____ (4:6–8).
- What is God's question to Jonah (4:9)?

- What is God's assessment of Jonah (4:10)?

God's chosen prophet did give the message of repentance to the "others" who would become believers, though he was not happy about it.

God allowed Jonah to be part of His plan to bring people to Him, but also used the event to teach Jonah a lesson about Himself. What do you think God was teaching Jonah while getting a message to a foreign people?

John the Revelator of prophecy and the global track

The apostle John wrote the book of Revelation between AD 95 and 100 from the Isle of Patmos, addressing the seven churches of Asia Minor. We will look at Revelation 13 and Revelation 18 to gain an understanding of unfulfilled prophecy that is on the global track—a message of warning to the people of all nations who will exist during the last seven years of Gentile power on the planet earth. Rebellion will be global. It will be very apparent when reading Revelation that all men are sinners who need a Savior. The first global rebellion led by Satan in the Garden of Eden against God and mankind will ultimately lead to the last global rebellion Satan will lead against Jesus and the saints (see Revelation 20).

Read Revelation 13. Note specifically where you see the concept of the whole world under the rule of a beast from the sea—who is a global ruler—and answer the following questions.

- Who is amazed by him (13:3)?

- Who worships him (13:4)?

- What kind of authority is given to this beast (13:7)?

- Who worships him (13:8)?

- Who is warned (13:9)?

- Another beast comes up, the false prophet (13:11; see also 19:20). What is he doing and to whom (13:12–13)?

- Who is deceived (13:14)?

- Who is marked (13:16)?

- If they can't buy or sell without his mark, what is he controlling (13:17)?

- Revelation 17:1–6 describes a great harlot riding a beast, representing a false religions system. Who has committed immorality with her (v. 2)?

- Whose blood is she drunk with (17:6)?

- Revelation 18 describes the world system of the antichrist. Who is described as participating with him (18:3)?

- Who are the three groups weeping at Babylon's destruction (18:9–17)?

- Who is told to rejoice over her and why (18:20)?

- In Revelation 19:19–21, who is under judgment? What is clearly told will happen in the future?

Application Truths from This Session

1. There is a righteous Judge who is coming to set up His global rule on the earth!

2. First Peter 4:7–8 warns us, "The end of all things is at hand; therefore be serious and watchful in your _____. And above all things have fervent love for one another." We are to prepare our garment to meet our Bridegroom.

3. Take time to thank the Lord Jesus for what He has done for you at the cross to save you for all of eternity.

4. Thank Him for the fact that He has given us *all* of His Word to prepare us for our future as believers and to reveal His complete plan for the world.

We don't want to be here for the time we have just seen described in Revelation 13, 17, 18. We are looking for the Rapture, our blessed hope, to be discussed in chapters 7–8.

4

THE LONG, WINDING ROAD
OF PROPHECY

Before He even said, "Let there be light," He had a plan for our redemption. . . . The Lamb of God was *identified, and His sacrifice was planned before Adam ever existed, before the Garden of Eden or the earth itself was formed,* before Satan himself was created.

The Last Hour, page 56, emphasis added

This part of the study will take us on a long road of prophecy that, although planned before the foundation of the world and creation, was actually spoken in the Garden, in Ur of the Chaldees, in Egypt, in the wilderness, in Jerusalem, in Babylon and in Asia Minor. The prophecies from those in the Garden to those in Revelation reveal the unfolding plan of God. We will also see that as the plan unfolded before the enemy, he attempted to thwart it all through history. But Scripture tells us he is doomed and his destiny is the lake of fire! We must read the end of the Book to discover this wonderful prophecy.

The first command in the Bible given in the form of a conditional prophecy is where the story of mankind begins.

Prophecies in the Garden

Read Genesis 2:16–17.
  What is the specific command given to Adam?

What prophecy or consequence is explicitly stated?

When was it fulfilled?

At the point of disobedience, Adam and Eve died spiritually. They were deceived by the serpent into thinking they could become gods (*elohim*), not realizing once they knew "evil" and good, they had no ability or power in and of themselves to avoid evil nor any ability to be truly "good."

Read Genesis 3:14–24. Look for the prophecies concerning the following:

Adam

Satan

Woman

The Seed of woman

Since these are the first prophetic words in the Bible, it is important to note that they had a literal and a spiritual fulfillment, as will be the case of future prophecies.

- Spiritual death occurred immediately in the Garden—they were expelled from the presence of God, indicating separation from God spiritually, as well as the loss of the physical presence of God and the intimacy it provided.
- The physical death of a living substitute to provide physical clothing for their bodies points to the need for an innocent blood substitute to cover the sins of the soul. Just as they needed clothing to cover their physical nakedness, they were spiritually naked before God as well.
- They began to experience pain and toil when tilling the ground and labor in childbirth and eventually physical death.

These prophecies in Genesis 2 and 3 are the beginning of the road that will lead to the salvation of man provided by the Son of God, literally, through His shed blood. He became our substitute two thousand years ago on a cross in Jerusalem. But there is more to study to see the unfolding plan of God in the Torah, the Prophets and the Writings of the Old Testament.

Prophecy Given in the Area of Mount Ararat in Turkey

Read Genesis 9:11, 21–27.
    What is the specific promise to Noah?

What is prophesied about Shem?

This declaration about Shem foreshadows the family God will use to produce the Seed of woman. The Seed of woman will be a descendant from the line of Shem, who was from Adam.

Prophecy Given in Ur of the Chaldees

Read Genesis 12:1–3 to see the prophecies made to Abram in Ur.

- to make him a great _____
- to bless him and make his _____ great
- to bless those who _____ him and curse those who _____ him
- to bless all the _____ of the _____ through Abram

These promises are about giving Abram *seed* (physical descendants), *blessing* and *land* to live on eternally (see Genesis 12, 15, 17).

The focus here is not only on Abram and his seed to come, but on the fact that through Abram and his offspring, all the world will be blessed. The Seed of woman, the prophesied Messiah of Israel, will be born into the Jewish nation.

Read Romans 9:3–5 below and highlight the parts that validate that the Messiah (Christ) would be a Jewish man from the nation of Israel. Also highlight the portion that indicates the Messiah is God.

For I could wish that I myself were accursed from Christ for my brethren, my countrymen according to the flesh, who are Israelites, to whom pertain the adoption, the glory, the covenants, the giving of the law, the service of God, and the promises; of whom are the fathers and from whom, according to the flesh, Christ came, who is over all, the eternally blessed God. Amen.

Prophecy to Isaac in Gerar

Read Genesis 26:2–5. List the promises or prophecies made to Isaac:

1. _____

_____

2. _____

_____

3. _____

_____

4. _____

_____

5. _____

_____

6. _____

_____

Prophecy to Jacob at Bethel

Read Genesis 28:12–28. List the promises given to Jacob:

1. _____

_____

2. _____

   _____

   _____

3. _____

   _____

   _____

Did you see land, seed/descendants and blessing like the promises to Abram?

Read Genesis 32:22–30. What was Jacob's name changed to as he was returning to the Promised Land to face his brother, Esau?

Prophecy of Jacob to His Twelve Sons in Egypt

Read Genesis 49:1–10. This is the final blessing of Jacob for his twelve sons and their seed for the "last days."

What did he prophesy would not depart from the tribe of Judah?

Shiloh, a term for the Messiah of Israel, would come from the tribe of Judah. That tribe was determined by God to be the tribe the kings of Israel were to come from until the Messiah Himself, who would be the King of kings! That was Jesus Christ, the Son of David, who would have an eternal kingdom. Remember, *Shiloh* means "He whose right it is"—it is a reference to the Messiah!

Prophecy Given to Balaam in Moab

Balaam, a Gentile prophet, was hired by the king of Moab to curse the nation of Israel. Numbers 22 records the conversation between Balaam and God, who warned Balaam not to go with the men from Moab. The king of Moab did not give up. This time, God told Balaam he could go with the men from Moab, but he could only speak what God told him. Balaam was unable to curse Israel and could only bless them.

Read Numbers 23:8–10. How does this prophecy relate to what God has promised Abram, Isaac and Jacob?

Read Numbers 24:5–8. How could these verses be prophesying about the Messiah?

Read Numbers 24:16–19.

- "A Star shall come out of _____."
- "A Scepter shall rise out of _____."
- He will "batter the brow of _____."
- "Edom shall be a _____."
- Seir, Edom's _____, shall also be a possession.
- One from Jacob will have _____.

This is prophesying that a King out of Jacob/Israel will have dominion. This is more prophecy about the Jewish Messiah, Jesus Christ, who will rule eternally.

Wilderness Prophecy Given to Moses

Read Deuteronomy 18:15–19. This prophecy was given on the east side of the Jordan before the second generation entered the Promised Land, just before the death of Moses. What were the people told about this prophet who would be raised up among them?

- He would be a prophet like _____ (v. 15).
- They were to *shemah*—or _____ — Him because God would put His words in His mouth (v. 15).
- If they did not listen to Him, God would _____ it of them (v. 19).

Now look at some passages from the Gospels:

- Matthew 17:5 says, "This is My beloved Son, in whom I am well pleased. _____ Him!" The disciples would recognize that Jesus was the Son and the Prophet Moses spoke of, the One who was coming to speak God's words to them as He revealed Himself to Israel—the One they were to hear/*shemah*.
- In John 4:25–26, Jesus told the Samaritan woman He was the Messiah who would declare all things to them—indicating that what He declared, they should listen to.
- In John 8:28, Jesus said He would speak the things the _____ taught Him.
- In John 12:49–50, Jesus said, "I have not spoken on My own authority; but the _____ who sent Me gave Me a command. . . . And I know that His command is _____ ." This is the real message of Jesus from the Father—everlasting life!

Prophecy to David in Jerusalem

Read 1 Chronicles 17:11–14.

One of David's sons would rule over the kingdom, and his throne would be established _____.

This is the promise to David, that he would have an eternal throne and kingdom through his seed, who would be Jesus the Messiah, born in the fullness of time to Mary of the house of David.

Luke 2:32 prophesied the child would be a light of revelation to the _____ and the glory of the people of _____—thus blessing all the families of the earth.

Prophecy to Isaiah in Jerusalem

Read Isaiah 11:1–5 below. The shoot from the stem of Jesse is the promised Messiah from Jesse's son David.

> There shall come forth a Rod from the stem of Jesse, and a Branch shall grow out of his roots. The Spirit of the LORD shall rest upon Him, the Spirit of wisdom and understanding, the Spirit of counsel and might, the Spirit of knowledge and of the fear of the LORD. His delight is in the fear of the LORD, and He shall not judge by the sight of His eyes, nor decide by the hearing of His ears; but with righteousness He shall judge the poor, and decide with equity for the meek of the earth; He shall strike the earth with the rod of His mouth, and with the breath of His lips He shall slay the wicked. Righteousness shall be the belt of His loins, and faithfulness the belt of His waist.

What part of this passage would occur at the first coming, the incarnation of Jesus?

What part of this passage will occur at His Second Coming?

Prophecy to Jeremiah in Babylon

Read Jeremiah 23:5–6. List the promises or prophecies.

- God will raise up to David a _____ of righteousness.
- He will reign as _____ and execute _____ and righteousness.
- In His days, _____ will be saved and Israel will dwell _____ .
- This is His Name: The Lord our _____ .
- His name is Jehovah (Lord)—the Messiah is Jehovah!

Prophecy to Daniel in Babylon

Read Daniel 9:24–27.

The timing of the coming of the Messiah is given in this short prophecy. There is a decree to rebuild the city after the captivity, and then 69 "sevens" would click off—a Jewish period of 483 years, or 173,880 days, until the Messiah is _____ (v. 26). Jesus was born in the exact time period predicted and was crucified at the end of the 69 sevens period.

This prophecy, written five hundred years before the birth of Jesus, predicted the exact time period of His death. It is proof that the Jewish Messiah has been born in time and has been "cut off"—killed. It is today largely ignored by rabbis who deny Jesus was the Messiah. It is too compelling!

Prophecy to Zechariah in Jerusalem

Read Zechariah 9:9–17.

- The King did come to Jerusalem lowly and riding on a
  _____ the first time.
- He will also appear a second time to fulfill verses 14–16—this
  time on a white horse from heaven described in Revelation 19.

This long, winding road has led from the Garden to Egypt to the wilderness, to the land of Israel, then to captivity in Babylon to Bethlehem and the birth of the Messiah, to Jerusalem and the death and resurrection of the Seed of woman—the One who would ascend into heaven from the Mount of Olives. There is yet more prophecy of His return! What a journey, and yet all the way, Satan attempted to destroy the Seed as each prophecy was made known.

A quick look at the attempts on the life of the Messiah will reveal a pattern of the enemy:

- Genesis 4, outside the Garden: Cain killed _____.
- Exodus 1, Egypt: Pharaoh had the _____ babies of the Hebrews drowned.
- Esther, Persia: Haman tried to have all Jews everywhere exterminated.
- Matthew 2, Bethlehem: King Herod ordered the murder of all _____ who were two years old and younger.
- Matthew 16:22: Satan was behind Peter, who did not want Jesus to die on the cross for the world.
- Zechariah 13:7–9: In the Tribulation, _____ of Israel will die.
- The Crusades, the Inquisitions, the Holocaust and the Tribulation are all attempts to wipe out the nation that must call the Messiah back to earth.

Do you see how Satan is so determined to wipe out the Jewish nation, with his grand scheme to abort the prophecies that will bring Jesus back and secure Satan's doom?

Application Truths from These Prophecies

God's plan:

1. Adam and Eve would have descendants, or seed.
2. They would have dominion over the earth—that is, land and blessing for obedience to His Word.
3. They were given free will, and because they listened to the lusts of the flesh and the lie of the Serpent, they became the very first two exiles from their home (land).
4. But they also received the promise that the Seed of woman would triumph over the Serpent and his seed; then would come redemption and restoration for those people who choose to believe these beautiful prophecies and promises.

Years later, God gave Abram the same promises:

1. He promised Abram a specific land with specific borders.
2. Abram would have seed or offspring to live on that land.
3. Abram had God's blessing.
4. However, to bless all the families of the earth, the one Seed of Abraham—the Messiah—must come and die. Then the families of the earth can receive eternal life and be blessed forever to live with Him and to rule and reign with Him.

Praise Him for His plan and the fact that He has revealed it in His Word!

The third element of blessing, land, also brings a comparison between the first man and the first patriarch. To Adam the whole earth was given, and he was told to fill it and subdue it. Abraham was only given a small portion of land on the east bank of the Mediterranean. But, while Adam's lot was bigger, Abraham's lot was the land of promise—the home of the city where God Himself dwells, the place where Immanuel walked the earth, the scene of the Savior's death, resurrection and ascension, the location where the Great Judge will return to His creation and the site of the eternal reign of the King of kings and Lord of lords.

The Last Hour, page 65

5

ISRAEL: STILL GOD'S CHOSEN PEOPLE

The Jews have a special relationship with the Lord and a distinct plan, but not a separate path to salvation. Everyone is saved through an individual acceptance of what Jesus did on the cross. Jews are not saved by following the law. Jews are not saved because they are Jews. They are, however, the only people who will experience a national salvation. This salvation will only come when revival spreads among the Jews who survive the Tribulation and individually commit themselves to the Lord.

The Last Hour, pages 86–87

In this study, we will examine from Scripture what God said about Israel and the reason He chose them, what He has to say about their rebellion and what He says about their national salvation, which most Christians do not realize will and must happen.

Romans 11:25–26—A Mystery

In Romans 11:25–26, Paul mentions a mystery. What is the mystery?

Paul specifically says this blindness has happened to Israel *until* the
_____ of the _____ has come in. And then all Israel
will be saved.

That has not happened yet, because the fullness of the Gentiles has not
yet "come in." Theologians believe this will happen when the last Gentile
has come into the Church, and then the Church—Jew and Gentile—
will be raptured out (see 1 Thessalonians 4:13–18). Then will follow the
Tribulation, which is designed for the salvation of Israel and the salvation of Gentiles left during the Tribulation. The fullness of the Gentiles
is connected with the salvation of Israel!

Back to the Beginning to Discover God's Plan

- Genesis 1–2: There were no nations, no ethnicities in the beginning, just the human race.
- Genesis 3: Man was given free will to choose to obey God, and
  man failed.
- Genesis 3–5: Cain killed Abel. Lamech was a bigamist and mur-
  derer. Mankind became violent.
- Genesis 6–9: God sent the Flood because of the violence of men
  and started over with Noah and his three sons—telling them to
  be fruitful and multiply and fill the earth.
- Genesis 10–11: Rebellion of mankind at the Tower of Babel occurred when it appeared Nimrod was trying to keep all the world
  united under his rule after the Flood. They did not scatter as God
  commanded, so God confused their languages, causing them to
  spread out, thus beginning the development of the nations and
  their boundaries.
- Genesis 12: This begins the story of Abraham and the covenant
  God made with him promising physical land with certain boundaries (Genesis 15), physical seed/descendants to live on the land, and

a blessing to him and to all the families of the earth. That blessing to the world would be the birth of a person who would come from heaven as the God-Man from one of Abraham's very descendants!

Why Did God Choose the Nation of Israel?

Read Deuteronomy 7:6–8 to discover why God says He chose Israel.

- He chose them to be a _____ for Himself, a _____ _____ (v. 6).
- "The LORD did not set His love on you nor choose you because you were more in _____ than any other people, for you were the _____ of all peoples; but because the LORD _____ you, and because He would keep the oath which He swore to your fathers" (vv. 7–8).

What can you learn about God from these verses?

Read Deuteronomy 9:4–7. What does God say they were not to think about themselves?

What are the two reasons given for driving out the nations (Gentiles)?

Read Deuteronomy 9, where God reminds Israel of their rebellious acts. List some of them:

The words of Isaiah 43:10–12 are spoken to Israel hundreds of years later in the land of Israel. What does God call Israel?

Why does He say He chose them?

Romans 9:4–5 lists eight unique privileges given to the nation of Israel by God:

1. Adoption as sons (see also Hosea 11:1)
2. The glory—visible manifestation of the presence of God (see also Exodus 40:34–38)
3. The covenants with Abraham, Jacob, Moses and David
4. The law
5. The Temple worship
6. The promises of an eternal Kingdom
7. The forefathers
8. The Messiah

Israel became the conduit for the revelation and preservation of God's word to the prophets, the promises of the Messiah to come and ultimately the Messiah Himself, who would bless *all* the families of the earth. This is why God chose Israel to record His written Word and to bring the Living Word, Jesus, into the world. Without belief in Jesus, individual Jews will not benefit from these privileges and blessings given them as a nation by God.

Did Israel Obey God and Become a Light to the Gentiles?

God came down to dwell in the Temple built by Solomon. First Kings 8 is the dedication prayer of Solomon. Verse 60 sums up the reason for Israel's existence and God's presence in His Temple. What is it?

At Solomon's death, God divided the kingdom of Israel into ten tribes in the north and two in the south. The reason was the idolatry of the people. This would lead to the Assyrian captivity of the Northern Kingdom and later the Babylonian captivity of the Southern Kingdom as well as the burning of Solomon's Temple and destruction of Jerusalem. But God was not finished with His chosen people.

When God warned them of the coming invasions, He *always* gave them a promise for their future. When they did go into captivity, He sent prophets with promises of hope—there would be a return to the land and a remnant to live on the land. They still have those promises today that call for a second return and a national salvation.

Jeremiah sent a letter from Jerusalem to the exiles in Babylon. Read Jeremiah 29.

- What did God tell them to do immediately (vv. 5–7)?

- What did God say about the prophets in their midst (v. 8)?

- How long did God say they would be there?

- What did God promise to do for them at the end of the seventy years?

- Why (v. 11)?

- What does verse 14 specifically promise Israel?

This is a prophecy that occurred after the seventy-year Babylonian captivity but was given during the captivity. They returned to the land, but they did not all seek Him and return to Him. When He sent His Son four hundred years after that captivity, they did not believe Him and rebelled once again. In AD 70 that generation was sent into worldwide captivity, scattered to the four corners of the earth.

Read Isaiah 41:8–10. What does God call Israel and say about them?

It shall come to pass in that day that the Lord shall set His hand again the second time to _____ the _____ of His people who are left, from Assyria and Egypt, from Pathros and Cush, from Elam and Shinar, from Hamath and the islands of the sea. He will . . . assemble the outcasts of Israel, and gather together the dispersed of Judah from the four _____ of the earth.

Isaiah 11:11–12

This is a promise to gather all of the nation of Israel a second time, which will be the last time and will occur at the Second Coming of Jesus because they will have been scattered once again at the midpoint of the Tribulation. They will never be scattered again. God will keep His promises!

What Promises Did God Make to Israel in Ezekiel?

Read Ezekiel 36. God addresses the mountains of Israel, the land.

- What does He tell the land to do and for whom (v. 8)?

- Why does God do this (v. 22)?

- Who is God speaking to now, and what will He do (v. 24)?

- What promises are in these verses (vv. 25–30)?

In Ezekiel 37, God tells Ezekiel to prophesy over the dry bones of Israel in the graves of the nations where they were scattered.

- What comes into the bones (v. 10)?

- How has Israel felt (v. 11)?

- List the promises to Israel:
  (vv. 11–14)

  (vv. 21–22)

- What will He make with them (v. 26)?

- Where will God dwell (v. 27)?

- Why is He doing this (v. 28)?

Israel was reestablished as a nation after 1,878 years—from AD 70 when scattered to 1948—and is now a recognized nation in the world. This has not happened to any other nation in the history of the world. They do not yet have the Spirit within them as a nation, nor is God yet dwelling among them as a nation, so these prophecies must be fulfilled in the future.

What Is the Spiritual Condition of Israel today?

Israel has been and still is the only nation in covenant with the God of heaven. We will look at the Scriptures that show they will have a "national salvation" that no other collective nation will have. We will see where they are today spiritually, how they will arrive at a national salvation and how that relates to the Second Coming of their Messiah, Jesus.

Read Hosea 3:4–5. Is Israel without a king or priesthood today?

Read Romans 11:1–5. How does Paul describe God's people, Israel?

The idea of a remnant of those who are truly committed to the one true Creator, the God of heaven and earth, is a principle taught from Noah to Lot to Elijah and will be true of "true Israel" in the end. After the call of Abraham and the covenant promises to him, the one true God of heaven and earth is known as the God of Abraham, Isaac and Jacob.

Read Micah 2:12–13. What does God say about the remnant of Israel?

How is this passage different from Hosea 3:4–5?

Read Matthew 23:37–39, where Jesus spoke before His death, "Jerusalem, Jerusalem"—referring to the very city where the Temple stood, to the religious leaders who taught in the Temple and to the people who had missed their "day of visitation" (see Luke 19:44).

- What could "your house" be a reference to? Could it have a double reference?

- What do they (the leaders of the nation and the people as well) have to do before Jesus returns to the nation of Israel to begin the millennial kingdom?

Now read Hosea 5:15–6:1–3.

- Who has returned to His place until the people of Israel acknowledge their guilt and seek His face?

- What condition will cause Israel to call on His name?

- Connect this action with Jesus' prophecy in Matthew 23:37–39. Who are they really acknowledging in Hosea 6:1–3?

Summary of the National Salvation of Israel

A remnant of Israel will come to belief in Jesus as their Messiah during the seven-year Tribulation.

Daniel 9:24 clearly states the purpose of the seventy-week period, which is 490 years. The sixty-ninth week ended with the crucifixion of the Messiah. The seventieth week is the final seven-year period, also known as Jacob's trouble and the Tribulation, which is still in the future. The full 490 years are designated for Daniel's people, the Jews and the Holy City, Jerusalem.

Daniel lists the six things that will be accomplished by the end of the seventieth week (notice, this prophecy is *not* to the Church, which was a mystery to the Old Testament prophets):

1. To finish the transgression
2. To make an end of sin
3. To make reconciliation for iniquity
4. To bring in everlasting righteousness
5. To seal up vision and prophecy
6. To anoint the most holy

These will be accomplished for Israel, not any other group, at the end of the seventieth week.

- These things will be true for only the nation of Israel in the Millennium because in their affliction, they as a nation call on the One they pierced (see Zechariah 12:10).

61

- They will confess their national sin and individual sin and mourn Him under much affliction, which will be the Tribulation (see Hosea 5:15). Their sin was the rejection of Jesus Christ!
- They will confess the sin of rejection by their forefathers as stated in Leviticus 26, calling on Him as stated in Hosea 6:1–3.
- This then fulfills the Day of Atonement, when they acknowledge the Lamb of God as Messiah, who atoned for their sins.
- Jesus said Israel won't see Him again until they say, "Blessed is He who comes in the name of the LORD!" (Matthew 23:39), which is acknowledging Jesus as Messiah, Lord, Savior and God of Israel.
- He will not return to this earth until they confess their national sin of rejection and call on Him.
- Zechariah 12 speaks of their refining, Zechariah 13 of their national cleansing and Zechariah 14 of the Second Coming to the Mount of Olives and their salvation.

Application Truths from This Session

Now we see why anti-Semitism is so rampant. Satan does not want Israel to have a national salvation. He wants to keep that prophecy from ever happening so he stays "safe" and on the loose—out of the lake of fire.

We must also remember that Acts 17:30–31 commands "all men everywhere to repent" because there is a fixed day in which God "will judge the world in righteousness" through the Man He has raised from the dead. All men must stand before Jesus Christ, the righteous Judge. He will be the substitute and Advocate for those who have claimed Him as Savior, or He will be the Judge who will condemn men for their sin of rejection. Jews will stand before Him, some as the remnant and true Israel whom He will never reject, and others will stand before the One they rejected. Be alert and be ready! No matter who you are, you need the Savior! With grateful hearts we bow at His feet and call Him King of kings.

Differences between Israel and the Church

Israel	The Church
Israel, the firstborn of God	The Church, Bride of Messiah
Born into a nation—physical birth	Born into a body—spiritual birth
Jews from the twelve tribes of Jacob	Jew and Gentile—one new man
The wife of Jehovah	The Bride of the Messiah, Jesus
Birthed the Messiah from the nation	Birthed at Pentecost by the Holy Spirit
Will repent after affliction of the Tribulation	Repentance to be "born again"
Will be rescued after the Tribulation by Jesus	Will be removed before the Tribulation
Four-fifths of the Bible is about Israel/nation	In the New Testament, 21 of the 27 books are letters to or history about the Church
A nation with literal borders and a capital	A priesthood of believers
Direct recipients of covenants	Grafted into the covenants
Had physical wars with enemy nations	Spiritual warfare
Physical Temple and sacrificial system	The spiritual temple of God
Judgment during the Tribulation	Bema (Judgment) Seat reward during the Tribulation
Jesus' farewell address to Israel (see Matthew 24)	Jesus' farewell address to disciples (see John 14–17—Upper Room)
Nations were "to come and see" God	Church is to go into the nations
Blessings are primarily physical/earthly	Blessings are primarily spiritual
Earthly Jerusalem is the focus	Heavenly Jerusalem is the focus
The nation is in unbelief but will believe	Must be "born again" to be a member
The Tribulation is to purge the unbelievers	No purging is necessary

6

THE DECEPTION OF
THE NATIONS

Satan deceives individuals in order to draw them away from God. He also has larger deceptions that operate on a global scale—a duplicitous metanarrative that he is foisting on the world. These global deceptions fall into two categories: the deception of the world and the deception of the nations. The deception of the world has to do with the rise of a global economy, a global religion and final world leader all will follow.

The Last Hour, page 97

I n this chapter of *The Last Hour,* Amir discusses the master deceiver, Satan, and the two categories of his deception—deception of the world and deception of the nations. This may seem like the same thing, but in his video teaching *Deception of the Nations,* Amir explains that the "world" includes the nation of Israel and all the Gentile nations, but the "nations" refers to the Gentile nations only, excluding Israel.

Satan has deceived the Gentile nations about the character of the God of Israel, about His choice of Israel, about the prophecies of their future and about their land. This deception of the Gentile nations is easily seen today in the attempt to eradicate history and furnish a new narrative. You will be looking to the Bible to see the truths about the nations of the world, the Arabs in particular, and the nations of Israel.

What Is the Distinction between the Nations and the Nation of Israel?

Read the following Scriptures and look for the distinction between the nations of the world and Israel or the whole world. See if you can tell what time period each verse is referring to, i.e. the Tribulation, the end of the Tribulation, the Millennium or after the new heaven and new earth.

Revelation 12:7–9

Isaiah 14:12 (about the fall of Lucifer)

Revelation 20:1–3

Revelation 20:7–9

Revelation 21:24

Isaiah 14:12 says Satan has "weakened the nations." Can you give an example of how he has done that in the past and even now with respect to God's will and plan for salvation and the coming of a Savior?

Deception #1: Israel Is Not God's People Anymore

Since Satan is the father of lies (John 8:44) and does not stand in the truth, he cannot tell the truth but is very good at mixing the truth with lies, enough to deceive and poison the minds of the nations about who God is and who His chosen people are. These lies indeed "weaken the Gentile nations." One way is to throw doubt on God's Word or to outright contradict it.

Read the following Scriptures and list the things God says about His chosen people.

Deuteronomy 4:7–8

Deuteronomy 7:7–8

Deuteronomy 7:17–24

Deuteronomy 14:2

Isaiah 49:14–16

Jeremiah 31:3
How much does God love Israel?

Haggai 2:7

Zechariah 2:8

Roman 11:1

God chose Israel, He loves them with an everlasting love, He disciplines those He loves, He is faithful to His word and He will keep His promises and oaths to the forefathers of the nation of Israel.

How does knowing all this about God and His character and faithfulness to His promises in the Old Testament encourage you and deepen your faith in Him today?

Deception #2: The Land's Real Name Is Palestine

Most Gentile Christians are deceived about the name of the land of Israel today because of the media, the maps in their Bibles and the lack of teaching by the Church about the nation of Israel. Satan has deceived not only the nations and their leaders but many in the Church today. We need to research the Bible and see what the Scriptures, not the maps, have to say about the name of the land. The word Palestine is never used in the Scriptures. That name was given to the land in AD 145 by Hadrian, a Gentile Roman emperor, not the Lord God of Israel. Satan wants to eradicate the name of Israel from the map (see Psalm 83).

Read the following Scriptures. What is the "land" specifically called?

1 Samuel 13:19

1 Chronicles 22:2

Ezekiel 37:11–12

Ezekiel 40:2; 47:18

Matthew 2:19–21

God Himself refers to "the land of Israel." This is the land of the patriarch Jacob, who was renamed Israel in Genesis 32.

- This physical land was promised to his descendants, his twelve sons known as the twelve tribes of Israel.
- God chose this nation to bring His Son and His written Word to the world to save those who will believe in His Son.

- The battle is for the souls of the Gentile nations as well as for the souls of the Jewish nation, as seen in the last chapter.
- Psalm 83 says that the neighboring nations of Israel want to wipe out her name forever.
- Second Corinthians 11:3–4 says that Satan deceives by his trickery and leads minds astray.

How has he done that today concerning the land of Israel and its rightful owners, according to the Bible? What is the opinion of most in the media today?

Deception #3: The Arabs Were There First

The conflict over the land today goes back to a family conflict with the other descendants of Abraham. They were assigned land, but Satan has deceived their descendants that those promises have either changed or been abrogated. You will look at the historical record in the Bible to see how this family feud plays out.

Genesis 1–11: There were no nations at first—only one race, mankind. Up to Noah, all men descended from Adam and Eve. After the Flood, all men descended from Noah's three sons. At the Tower of Babel, men had decided to follow their own gods and wanted to make a name for themselves. God came down and confused their languages, and this began the development of the Gentile nations and their cultures.

Genesis 12: Abraham was from Ur of the Chaldees and was called out to be the father of a great nation that we later know as the nation of Israel.

Abraham basically has two branches to his family—Isaac and Jacob, who begat the twelve tribes called the sons of Israel; and Ishmael, who fathered twelve princes, who today are the Arab nations. As well, Esau's descendants and those descended from Lot—"cousins" of Israel—are among the Arab nations today.

So, who was there first? Or who was assigned this land?

Read the following Scriptures and see if you can answer the question above.

Genesis 13:14–17
   Who is addressed, where are they and how long are the promises for?

Genesis 16:8–16
   List the promises made to Hagar, the Egyptian mistress of Sarai:

   1.

   2.

   3.

   4.

   5.

   6.

Genesis 25:13–18
   Where were the Ishmaelites assigned to live?

   Do you know where this is today? Were they ever assigned the land of Canaan, which became the land of Israel when God made His covenant with Abraham, Isaac and Jacob?

Abraham's other sons

The descendants of Ishmael represent a portion of the Arabic peoples. After the death of Sarah, Abraham fathered six more sons by Keturah. Read Genesis 25:1–4. List their names below.

1. _____

2. _____

3. _____

4. _____

5. _____

6. _____

Where did he send them to live (v. 6)?

One of Keturah's sons is Midian, the father of the Midianites of Saudi Arabia. Moses' wife, Zipporah, was a Midianite who believed in the God of Abraham, Isaac and Jacob. What can be gleaned from this is that the sons of Keturah, Esau, Ishmael and Lot sometimes intermarried with the sons of Israel and with each other.

Read Genesis 28:13–15, which describes when Jacob fled to Haran from Esau. List the promises God gave Jacob at this point in time, before he fathered the twelve sons:

Verse 13

Verse 14

Verse 15

Jacob called the place where he received these promises Bethel, the house of God.

Read Genesis 28:9 and 36:3. What do you learn about Esau's wives?

Read Genesis 36:6–7. Where did Esau go and why?

Esau married an Ishmaelite and Canaanites as well. His descendants multiplied, became wealthy and moved to the east of the sons of Israel. Esau's descendants became known as the Edomites and lived in the area of Petra, which was later taken over by the Nabateans, another clan of Arabic descent. The Edomites moved into Judea when the Jews were taken into Babylonian captivity. These sons of Abraham have indeed wanted to claim the land God promised to Isaac and Jacob's descendants.

Nehemiah was concerned about Jerusalem and the escaped captives. He requested to return to the land to help rebuild the walls of Jerusalem. Read Nehemiah 1:9. What did Nehemiah remind God about Jerusalem?

Nehemiah did return and was met with resistance. Read Nehemiah 2:17–20. Who was there in Jerusalem giving Nehemiah resistance?

Nehemiah knew that the God of Israel had chosen to place His name in Jerusalem. He claimed the promises and the Word of God that he knew as a servant of the Living God of Israel.

In summary, Scripture shows that God promised a certain real estate to the sons of Israel and gave many more areas of land to the other descendants of Abraham. There are Arabs living in Egypt, Saudi Arabia, Iraq, Syria, Lebanon and Jordan today. They have been given a greater portion of land by God than what they are in dispute over in the Golan and Gaza. But Satan wants God's most holy spot, the Temple Mount, and the land of Israel. The battle will heat up before Jesus returns!

Deception #4: The Occupation Is the Problem

This deception spawned by the media has only been a problem since 1948, when Israel became a nation. One only has to look at the history from AD 70 to 1948 to see there was no occupation of the land and no claim by the Arabs until the Jews were approved by the UN to go to their homeland. This deception is so recent that the generation who saw Israel become a nation is still alive today to testify to the lies and deception that have been foisted on the nation of Israel by the enemy.

Deception #5: Peace in the Middle East Is Possible

This deception is also a modern deception that the nations have been led to believe. Since 1948, Israel has had to fight, and literally, God has miraculously won battles for them to remain a nation on their land. Jews today know there is no explanation for these victories but God. However, there is no prophecy in the Bible that says there will be peace in the Middle East before the return of the Prince of Peace, Jesus the Messiah.

Read Luke 19:41–44. What does Jesus say about peace in this passage?

Read Matthew 24:6–7. What does Jesus say about wars?

Read Luke 21:24. What does Jesus say about Jerusalem?

Read Daniel 9:24–27. This prophecy is about a false peace treaty that is broken at the midpoint of the Tribulation. It lasts only three and a half years. Then the Jews will flee Jerusalem and await their Messiah.

Daniel 2 recounts Nebuchadnezzar's dream of a statue representing the Gentile empires that will rule over Israel until the coming of the Stone to smash the entire statue and set up His own Kingdom of peace and righteousness.

Daniel 2:45 says that God made known to King Nebuchadnezzar what would take place in the future. This dream is a literal timeline of four major world powers from 605 BC until the coming of the Stone, Jesus, from heaven. These four empires are Babylon, Media/Persia, Greece and Rome, which is the last empire that divides and reconfigures in a ten-toe stage before the coming of the Stone. This is the "Times of the Gentiles," which will end when the Messiah comes back.

Read Joel 3:1–3. What is this passage describing about the nations/ Gentiles? This is when Jesus returns to earth.

Application Truths from This Session

1. Satan is in the business of deceiving nations as well as individuals. We must be alert and watchful to his schemes, especially when it comes to deception about the last days.

2. Gentile empires will rule the earth until the Messiah of Israel, Jesus of Nazareth, returns to smash the statue of evil empires and set up His Kingdom of peace, ruling with a rod of iron!

3. Until then, we must know the truth of the Word of God and know the hope that is ours as a free gift through the blood of Jesus Christ.

4. We should pray for the peace of Jerusalem and the soon return of Jesus and warn that Jesus will return as the Savior or the Judge.

5. We should love the ones that God loves—the nation of Israel and all people everywhere!

Maranatha! Come, Lord Jesus!

7

RAPTURE: THE GREAT
MYSTERY

Bible prophecy is a mystery rather than a secret. What a huge difference there is between the two! A secret is exclusionary. . . . A mystery is inclusionary: Understanding is available to every one of us who takes the time to discover it. Unlike a well-kept secret, a mystery does not remain hidden. Instead, it is a truth that transforms from shadow to substance. In the past, this transformation happened as God revealed more of His truth as Scripture was written. Today, this transformation typically takes place when we study and learn. We may think we understand something as it is, but then God shows more of His truth, and reality materializes out of the haze.

The Last Hour, page 120

The Greek word for mystery, *musterion*, means something known by God but not yet revealed. The Rapture has always been a known and planned event by God, but not revealed to the Old Testament prophets because the Rapture concerns the Church, which was also a mystery to the Old Testament prophets. It is important to understand that Israel will *not* be raptured out as a nation. That is why the Rapture of the Church was not revealed to Israel.

As we will see, the Rapture is an event for the Church-age believers only—that is, those who have died since Acts 2 and those who will be alive when Jesus comes for His Bride. It is a separate event from the Second Coming or glorious appearing of Jesus at the end of the Tribulation. We will observe the Rapture Scriptures in this chapter and in the next chapter as well, comparing the Rapture with the Second Coming.

What Are the Mysteries in the New Testament?

Read the following Scriptures and list the mystery found in each:

Colossians 2:2

Ephesians 3:6

Ephesians 5:31–32

1 Corinthians 15:51–52

Romans 11:25–26

How do these verses all relate to each other?

Where Is the Word *Rapture* Used in the New Testament?

The Greek word *harpazo* is translated "caught up" in the English and "rapturo" in Latin. *Harpazo* means to be snatched away suddenly, removed from one place to another, taken by force. We will observe some of the places *harpazo* is used in the New Testament. List who is removed and where they are taken in each of these passages.

Acts 8:39–40

2 Corinthians 12:2

Jude 23

Revelation 12:5

The Clearest Rapture Passage Is 1 Thessalonians 4:13–18

The Thessalonians were new believers whom Paul spent three weeks with before he was forced to leave by persecuting Jews. He wrote them 1 and 2 Thessalonians to answer their questions and give them hope for their future.

Read 1 Thessalonians 4:13–18 and answer the following questions:

• Who rises first?

- Who is "caught up"—raptured—with them?

- Where does this take place?

- Who are they meeting?

- What is the comfort given at the end of the passage?

Read 1 Corinthians 15:51–52. The mystery disclosed is that not all will sleep or die, but all will be changed from mortal bodies that die to bodies that will never die again, imperishable bodies.

- How does verse 52 seem to be describing the Rapture, or catching up?

- Who is raised when the trumpet sounds?

- Who are the "we who will be changed"?

The sting of death is taken from the dead who are raised to immorality because they will never die again. The sting of death is also taken from those who are alive and get a changed immortal body because they never have to experience death of their body!

What is the exhortation in 1 Corinthians 15:58?

This promise is for believers in Jesus (the Church made up of Jews and Gentiles).

- They will never die again.
- If alive at the Rapture, their bodies will be transformed into glorified bodies in an instant (see Philippians 3:20–21)!
- A glorified body will never die, will never experience sickness, will never age and will be able to enter heaven—immortal, imperishable forever!

For we know that if our earthly house, this tent, is destroyed, we have a building from God, a house not made with hands, eternal in the heavens. For in this we groan, earnestly desiring to be clothed with our habitation which is from heaven, if indeed, having been clothed, we shall not be found naked. For we who are in this tent groan, being burdened, not because we want to be unclothed, but further clothed, that mortality may be swallowed up by _____.

2 Corinthians 5:1–4

Paul indicates our physical, mortal bodies are tents—and temporary ones at that! We groan in these temporary tents that experience aging and death. We are incomplete at death because we are separated from the body He gave us, so we long for that body, that clothing, that will *live* and never die or age. He promises that very body to those who accept His sacrifice for our sins.

For our citizenship is in heaven, from which we also eagerly wait for the Savior, the Lord Jesus Christ, who will _____ our lowly body that it may be conformed to His _____ body, according to the working by which He is able even to subdue all things to Himself.

Philippians 3:20–21

Our resurrection bodies are guaranteed because of this verse and the fact that Jesus has a resurrected body.

- Jesus' physical body was not in the tomb (see Matthew 28:6).
- Jesus' resurrection body was flesh and bones (see Luke 24:39).
- Disciples were able to touch His body (see John 20:27–28).
- Jesus ate with disciples after His resurrection (see John 21:12–13).
- Jesus' body could defy gravity and laws of nature (see Acts 1:9–11).

Read John 14:1–3 and explain why this passage spoken to the disciples by Jesus before His death is also viewed as referring to the event known as the Rapture. Remember, this is to the disciples who would become some of the first members of the Church, the Bride of Christ.

- Where does Jesus tell the disciples He is going?

- What is He going to do?

- What is His promise?

Jesus promised to prepare a place for them and us in the Father's house and to return to take them to be with Him. They died two thousand years ago, along with thousands over the centuries. They will be the ones He raises first, and then He will change those who are alive. This is a promise exclusively for the Church, including those who will die before He returns.

Promises to the Church about the Wrath of God

The New Testament also promises the Church will be removed from the wrath to come. Read the following verses and note what the promise in each is.

1 Thessalonians 1:10

1 Thessalonians 5:9

Revelation 3:10

The removal of the Church before the wrath of the Lamb (see Revelation 6) was not prophesied in the Old Testament, but there are Old Testament foreshadowings of the idea of the removal of God's people before the judgment of God on unbelievers. In the Old Testament, who were those who were removed or taken?

Genesis 5:24

2 Kings 2:11–12

Enoch was a Gentile and Elijah was a Jew. They are symbolic patterns of Jewish and Gentile believers in the Church who will be raptured or removed physically, never to see death.

Calling the Ambassadors Home

Read 2 Corinthians 5:20. The role of the Church collectively and individually is one of ambassadors. What words does Paul use to convey the urgency of the job?

Read pages 132–133 in *The Last Hour*.

- List the description of an ambassador given by Amir.

- Why is an ambassador called home?

- How does that relate to the Church?

When the war begins for control of the world by Satan, the Church will be removed. This will begin the seventieth week of Daniel, which is prophesied for the cleansing and the salvation of the nation of Israel. The 144,000 and the two witnesses and many others will sound the trumpet and warn the age is coming to a close. The Jews who come to belief will become the new ambassadors of Jesus to get the truth out to Israel and the rest of the world. Time is short—the Day is approaching (see Hebrews 10:26)!

Application Truths from This Session

1. The question is, Are you part of the Church now?
2. Have you accepted His finished work on the cross so that you now have His Holy Spirit living within you?
3. If you are, you will be part of the Rapture, either raised from the dead or caught up if you are alive and remain till He comes. That is your blessed hope and comfort! Be certain of your future!

8

RAPTURE: THE GREAT GATHERING

God is also a gatherer of people. . . . There will come a time when Jesus will return to gather His Church to Himself. This is the promise of a Rapture that will take place to protect the Bride of Christ from the impending wrath of God.

The Last Hour, page 135

The Church and Wrath Do Not Mix

Read 1 Thessalonians 1:10 and 1 Thessalonians 5:9. Paul tells the church at Thessalonica two things to answer their questions about the future. List them below.

1. _____

2. _____

Since God's wrath or indignation is never said to be hell in the Scriptures, the wrath He is referring to—for which the Church is *not* destined—must be a judgment other than eternal punishment. God does tell the nation of Israel there will come a time called Jacob's trouble that is like no other time ever in the past but is yet to come. Jesus refers to this same time period in Matthew 24. This is referring to the seven-year Tribulation. Those who have not placed their faith in Jesus Christ will be "left behind" at the time of the Rapture. Those left here, Jew and Gentile, will face the judgments described in Revelation 6–9.

- Whose wrath is it according to Revelation 6:15–17?

- Whose wrath is it according to Revelation 12:12?

- In Revelation 3:10, how is this time period described and who is it coming upon?

This promise was specifically given to the church at Philadelphia, but they did not live to see the Tribulation, so this testing to come on the whole earth is still future and must be the Tribulation period that Jesus will keep the Bride from.

The Rapture: A Logistical Breakdown

Let's look at the *harpazo* passage given to the Thessalonians to determine the progression or order of the event called the Rapture, or the great gathering.

Read 1 Thessalonians 4:13–18.

- What is Paul's concern (v. 13)?

- Who is God bringing with Him (v. 14)?

- Who is Paul identifying with (v. 15)?

- What does he say about this group?

- Who descends with a shout and the voice of an archangel and trumpet of God (v. 16)?

- Who will rise first?

- Who is caught up with them?

- Where are they caught up (*harpazo*, raptured) to?

- Who do they meet, and where is the meeting?

- What are they to do with these words?

The Thessalonians were concerned about those who died as believers in Jesus. They are clearly told that those who died will return with the Lord Jesus to have their souls reunited with their bodies, which will be raised from the dead. Then those alive on earth will be caught up to meet the Lord Jesus and the dead, now-resurrected saints to be with the Lord _____ (v. 17).

First Corinthians 15:51–52 also describes the Rapture by telling the Corinthians that there is a mystery being revealed to them.

- What is the mystery?

- If not all die, what will happen to all believers who are alive?

The New Testament believers, the Church, who have died since Pentecost will be resurrected, and those alive will be changed! This will be the great gathering in the air to go to the Father's house—the entirety of Church-age believers will be together for the first time in two thousand–plus years and will always be with the Lord. This is the time of the Bema Seat judgment, when individuals stand before Jesus and receive rewards for deeds done after salvation. This will be at the Father's house—heaven. Daniel's seventieth week will be ongoing during this time on earth.

From these passages, we can extrapolate some reasons for the Rapture, or the rescue of the Church:

- To remove or rescue the Church believers from the wrath to come on the whole world.
- To resurrect those believers from Pentecost, described in Acts 2, who died.
- To reunite their souls with their resurrected bodies.
- To unite those who died believing in Jesus with those who are alive at His coming.
- To take the Church to the Father's house to be with Him and to reward the Bride at the Bema Seat.

All of these purposes can be seen in 1 Thessalonians 4:13–18; 1 Corinthians 15:51–52; and John 14:1–3.

Two Extreme Views Concerning the Rapture

Chuck Missler warned of two extreme views of the Rapture we need to take to heart.

1. Rapture mania, or date setting. We do not know the day or the hour (see Matthew 24:44).
2. Rapture paralysis—particularly in American churches, this is a guilt that there is persecution of the Church in the rest of the world and not here. Confusion about the Rapture comes with this view.[1]

The Rapture versus the Second Coming

The Rapture is the event when Jesus comes for His Church to remove her from the wrath to come.

1. Chuck Missler, *The Rapture: Christianity's Most Preposterous Belief* (Coeur d'Alene, Idaho: 2014), n.p., Kindle.

The Second Coming, as we will see, is a separate event after the Tribulation, when Jesus comes with the Church to remove the Antichrist, the false prophet and Satan so He can set up His millennial kingdom.

Rapture	Second Coming
1 Thessalonians 4; 1 Corinthians 15; John 14:1–3	Zechariah 14; Matthew 24; Revelation 19
Coming for the Bride (1 Thessalonians 4)	Coming with the Bride (Revelation 19)
A Mystery in the Old Testament (1 Corinthians 15:51–55)	Clearly revealed in Daniel 7:14
Coming in the air to take His Bride	Coming to the earth/Mount of Olives
Coming with the souls of the dead in Christ	Coming with the resurrected Bride
Not seen—in the twinkling of an eye	All the tribes/earth will see and mourn
No judgment of unbelievers	Judgment of the Antichrist, the false prophet and the unbelievers
No signs to precede it—any moment	Many signs before—seals, trumpets, bowls, the Antichrist, darkness, etc.
Shout, clouds, no angels mentioned	Coming with hosts of heaven, His Bride, souls of Old Testament saints and Tribulation saints
Admonition—Be steadfast, immovable, working	Admonition—Be alert, watching

The Rapture and the Second Coming are at least seven years apart; one was a mystery, one was not. The coming of the Son of Man is clearly taught in Daniel 7 and in the prophetic Psalms as well as in Isaiah, Hosea, Zechariah and Amos. The visible coming of Messiah was not a mystery in the Old Testament; but the Church, Jew and Gentile in one body, to get out the good news of the Gospel was a mystery and was never prophesied to be part of the sixty-nine weeks of Daniel nor part of the seventieth week of Daniel.

Is that hope and comfort to you as a believer? Read 1 Peter 4:3–18 and search your heart, looking for behavior that is pleasing to God or goes against the will of God, and then confess it, readying yourself to meet the Savior either in death or in the air!

What Did the Early Church Believe about the Rapture?

There is no clear consensus or teaching until the 1800s. The Dark Ages and the Catholic Church had stifled the study of Scripture by the common people. They did not believe in a literal thousand-year millennial kingdom, though the early believers did in the first and second centuries. They often thought they were in the throes of the Tribulation because of the persecution from various emperors, so they did believe the return was near! Were they hoping to be raptured out at the midpoint? But it is clear from early writings that some did believe in a pre-Tribulation Rapture. This belief is *not* a new belief since John Darby, as is erroneously taught by some today.

- Irenaeus, student of Polycarp, student of John the Revelator, believed an Antichrist would reign three and a half years and seat himself in the Temple (burned in his day); then the Lord will return with the clouds. It is unclear whether he expected a pre-, mid- or post-Tribulation Rapture.
- In AD 270, Victorinus, bishop of Petau, wrote of the Tribulation and the Church not here.
- In AD 373, Ephraem the Syrian wrote of the Church being gathered before the Tribulation.
- In northern Italy in AD 1260, Brother Dolcino used *rapture* in his writings. It was not an unknown word.
- In 1827, John Darby and others began to study the Scriptures for themselves, particularly prophecy. They were dispensational in their theology, separating the Church from Israel, unlike the theology of the Reformation and the Catholic Church.
- In 1832, a young Scottish girl had a vision of a partial Rapture at the midpoint of the Tribulation and warned people of the need to be ready. She did not teach pre-Tribulation, as some say today.

Application Truths from This Session

1. The Church is promised that Jesus will return for the living and will raise the dead in Christ at the same time to protect the Church from the wrath to come on the whole world.

2. The promise to the Church is to be delivered from the "wrath to come"—God's *za'am*, or indignation—which is against unbelieving Israel and the world.

3. The pattern in the Word of God is deliverance from the judgment or wrath—seen when God delivered Noah from death in the Flood and Lot from death and the judgment of Sodom and Gomorrah.

4. The meeting "in the clouds" will be an invisible event, but the Second Coming "with the clouds" will be visible to every eye.

9

THE ANTICHRIST:
THE MAN OF LAWLESSNESS

The spirit of the Antichrist began back in the Garden of Genesis 3 and has been moving, scheming and growing ever since. As we look at our culture today, we see his rebelliousness everywhere. Sometimes this rebelliousness is overtly anti-God; other times it is simply a thread of a lie woven into a tapestry of truth. As time moves on, it will not always be easy to discern truth from falsehood. We may not know who the Antichrist will be, but we do need to know what he is all about. This is why the emphasis should be less on the Antichrist himself and more on the lawlessness that is surrounding him. . . . He is only a by-product of a long line of lawlessness that began in the Garden and culminates in his rise to power. The Antichrist will not produce lawlessness; the mystery of lawlessness produces the Antichrist.

The Last Hour, pages 146–147

The Mystery of Lawlessness

Read 2 Thessalonians 2:3–4. What does "the man of lawlessness" do?

Read 2 Thessalonians 2:7. What do you learn about the "mystery of lawlessness"?

God is about righteousness, the proper way for man to live, which is by the righteous ways of God. Satan is about the very opposite—lawlessness, going against God's righteous laws and behavior. Satan is the father of lies, who comes to steal peace and life, kill humanity and destroy every good thing in his wake.

So, What Is the Antichrist and His Message?

First John 2:18 says, "Children, it is the last hour; and just as you heard that antichrist is coming, even *now* many antichrists have _____ ; from this we know that it *is* the last hour" (NASB, emphasis added).

While there is one final Antichrist to come, many have come in the past. Many scholars believe that Satan does not know who that final one will be, but he has had many candidates in the past who oppose God, His chosen nation, Israel, the Word of God and particularly the doctrine of the deity of Jesus.

So what will the message of the Antichrist be?

Read 1 John 2:22. Write down what you learn from this passage about his message.

The spirit of his message is here today, taught in the cults. They will first and foremost deny the deity of Jesus Christ and the doctrine of the Trinity, which is even taught in the Old Testament.

Read Isaiah 44:6. List the persons of the Trinity that are mentioned.

Read Isaiah 48:16 and list the persons of the Trinity mentioned.

Jehovah says He is the First and the Last. Who says the same thing in Revelation 1:8, 17 and Revelation 22:13?

Read Isaiah 14:14. The mystery of lawlessness began with Lucifer, who wanted to ascend above the heights of the clouds and be like the _____ _____! He wanted worship!

The message of the Antichrist will become more and more the polarized opposite of the Bible as the end draws near. Truth will be flipped on its head. Even today, there are those who believe the Bible was corrupted and that Lucifer is the true light and that Jews and Christians have changed the original truth. They are believing the delusional lies of Satan.

When Is the Antichrist Coming?

Read 2 Thessalonians 2:1–4. Specific events happen in a specific order before the Antichrist is revealed. List them:

1. _____

2. _____

What will the man of lawlessness do that will "reveal him" (v. 4)?

Since there is no Temple today in Jerusalem, what must happen for verse 4 to happen?

Why Is the Antichrist Coming?

Read 2 Thessalonians 2:9–12. How are those who are deceived described?

Amir writes,

> The Antichrist is coming to step into the void left by the rejection of Christ. The people of this world turned their backs on the truth of God and accepted the falsehoods of the liar and deceiver. . . . The Antichrist is coming to be received by those who refused to receive Christ.
>
> *The Last Hour*, page 153

Read John 1:10–11. How was Jesus received by His own countrymen?

The Antichrist, who is backed by Satan, will be able to tap into three desires of mankind:

1. The desire for government to provide a system of prosperity and equality for all
2. The desire for worldwide unity
3. The desire for global peace and security

Let's take a look at Scriptures that indicate this is how the Antichrist will win the world over.

Read Revelation 13:3 (NASB).

- The beast is the Antichrist who receives a _____ wound
  but is _____.
- The whole earth is _____ and follows after him.

It may be that this miraculous healing causes the whole earth to think this man has god-like qualities.

Revelation 13:4 says that the beast has the authority of the _____ (Satan), and the people worship the dragon and the beast—open Satan worship accepted by the global community. The Antichrist clearly has them deceived with his power and that of Satan, who they think is the true light!

Revelation 13:6 says the mouth of the beast speaks blasphemies against _____. Now more of his message is discernible. He will most likely make promises that he claims only he can bring to pass, and will claim that God has never done such a thing in the past nor did Jesus. He will be the ultimate blasphemer and liar, and many will fall for it, hoping for peace, security and prosperity.

Revelation 13:8 says all on the earth will worship him whose names are not written in the _____ of _____.

Daniel 9:27 indicates this Antichrist will make a covenant with Israel (the many) promising peace, but he will not keep his words and will break that covenant at the midpoint.

Revelation 13:7 says the Antichrist will have authority over whom?

The Antichrist will be worshiped in place of God. He will provide for those who take his number, and in a sense, if they put their faith and loyalty in him, he will make promises to them—possibly even tell them that God cannot provide eternal life but he can—using his own miraculous healing to deceive the masses.

Antichrist means "against Messiah (*Christos*)" or "in place of Messiah." The Old Testament has many passages that are called Messianic passages that describe what the Messiah will accomplish for Israel and the world. In some cases, the Antichrist will try to mimic those things, and in others, he will be the exact opposite.

Read Jeremiah 23:5–6 (NASB).

- Messiah will be a righteous branch of David.
- Messiah will reign as _____ and act _____.
- "In His days Judah will be _____, and Israel will live
  _____."
- His Name will be The LORD Our Righteousness.

According to 2 Thessalonians 2:4, the Antichrist will claim to be _____ in the rebuilt Jewish temple, putting himself in place of God.

In summary:

- The Antichrist will reign as king of the new world order.
- He will promise Israel she will be safe and secure because of his peace covenant.
- He will claim to have extraordinary wisdom, able to solve difficult problems.
- He will be lawless, *not* righteous; he will mimic what he can and lie about it all.

Where Will the Antichrist Come From?

Revelation 13:1 says the beast/Antichrist rises from the _____, which is a symbol of the Gentile world.

Daniel 2 describes a statue of four parts. The statue is in reality a timeline of the four major world empires who ruled the known earth—Babylon, Media/Persia, Greece and Rome. The last and final empire in the statue dream is the Roman Empire. The two legs represent the division of the Roman Empire that occurred between the East and the West beginning in AD 364. The feet and toes of clay and iron represent the last empire to rule the earth before the Stone from heaven smashes those Gentile empires to dust and the Kingdom without end is set up, that of the Messiah. This ten-toe stage corresponds to the ten horns seen on the fourth beast of Daniel 7 and the single beast seen in Revelation 13.

Daniel 7 describes four beasts that parallel the statue but with an added detail. It describes ten horns, parallel to the ten toes on the statue, which are on the fourth beast. Another "little horn" comes up among the ten, for a total of eleven horns. The "little horn" grows strong and uproots three of the ten and takes over the whole beastly system. This is the Antichrist coming from that revived Roman system. Thus, this last world ruler comes from the Gentile world to broker a peace covenant with Israel and is from that last empire, which means he will come from the Roman Empire, which is Europe today.

Read the dream in Daniel 7:9–14 and the interpretation in Daniel 7:15–28 and answer the following questions.

- The little horn was speaking what?

- What happens to him?

- Who comes in the clouds?

- What is He given?

- What do you learn about the saints in verse 18?

- What period of time is this describing, according to verse 19?

- How is this "king," or little horn, described in verses 23–26? Don't leave anything out.

- Who has dominion in the end?

- Do you see parallels with the beast in Revelation 13? List them.

This vision made Daniel exhausted and sick for days (see v. 28). He had just learned of one who would prosper for a time, who would destroy mighty men and holy people, who would deceive and even oppose the true Prince of Peace, yet he was told this little horn would be slain and go to the fire.

Read Revelation 19:20. Where is the beast sent? How does this parallel Daniel 7?

The Stone of Daniel 2 and the Son of Man of Daniel 7 is Jesus Christ the Savior, Messiah of the New Testament and the very one the book of Revelation is about.

A Modern Foreshadowing of the Antichrist

Hitler is one of the many men Satan has prepared, since he does not know when God will allow his "son" to take the reins of the earth for a "short time."

- Hitler was planning a Third Reich—a thousand-year reign.
- Hitler came from Germany, part of the old Roman Empire, the fourth beast of Daniel 7.
- Hitler was a mesmerizing orator.
- Hitler went from an insignificant person to worldwide power.
- Hitler was deep into the occult and wanted worship.

The picture of the little horn in Daniel and Revelation fits him, but he is history. And one worse than Hitler is to come on the scene, one who will rule during a time like never seen before on planet earth.

Be alert, be watchful and be about the Lord's business until the last trumpet for the Church sounds!

Application Truths from This Session

1. We need to know the truth of the Word so we are able to discern error when we hear it.
2. The false message of the Antichrist will be that he has the truth, he is the way and life will be given to mankind by obedience to him.
3. Part of his message may be that he now can give others eternal life because of his "return from the bottomless pit"—he and Lucifer may promise eternal life to all who follow him.
4. His message will also be blatant denial of the deity of Jesus Christ, as he is coming in the place of the true Son of God to sit on God's holy mountain/sacred space in Jerusalem as the savior of the world.

5. Revelation 13:18 calls for wisdom to understand the beast and his system. The Hebrew word for *wisdom* is *hokmah,* which points to the skill of a craftsman and the experience of counselors and is a word related to experience and efficiency. We need that God-given wisdom today, and certainly those living in the days of the Antichrist will need to seek this wisdom and knowledge and experience supplied only by the Holy Spirit. This is the wisdom that comes from above from the Word of God and leads one to godly living.

10

THE ANTICHRIST: ROLLING OUT THE RED CARPET

God has alerted the world of the coming man of lawlessness. He has clued us in as to his identity and origin. Furthermore, the Bible overflows with warnings against abandoning the Lord, plunging into sensuality, neglecting the helpless or relishing unrighteousness. When we look around, however, that is often all we see. The world is ignoring God's warnings, ascending step-by-step to the top of the skyscraper to take its plunge. The continent leading the march toward the end is Europe.

The Last Hour, page 163

Europe: Modern-Day Babylon

In the book, Amir describes how ancient Babylonian symbols can be seen in Europe today under the nose of Europeans who do not recognize them. The following is a summary of some of those symbols. These symbols are seen today and are very old symbols that are mentioned in the Bible!

- The European flag with twelve stars on a blue background is a possible reference to the Queen of Heaven.

- The symbol of a woman riding a beast has been taken as the symbol of the European Union. This symbol is based on the Greek myth of Europa's rape by a bull who was actually Zeus. This myth is the origin of the name of the continent of Europe and is a prevalent symbol today in Europe.

  The woman riding a bull is seen on German notes, on paintings in Berlin, on German EQ coins, on a British stamp, on European Central Bank notes and in sculptures at the European Parliament building in Brussels.

- The altar of Zeus brought from Pergamum is now in Berlin in the Pergamum Museum, which also houses the remains of the Ishtar Gate from Babylon.

- A move toward European unification is just a very old desire of Satan that started at Babel, a desire that is still alive and well.

Where Is the Queen of Heaven Referenced in the Bible?

The only two references in the Bible to the Queen of Heaven are in the book of Jeremiah. Jeremiah wrote to the people of Judah and Jerusalem before they went into Babylonian captivity. He also wrote to some of those left in Jerusalem who wanted to go to Egypt, against the strong warning of Jeremiah.

The two references to the Queen of Heaven are in Jeremiah 7, written before the Babylonian captivity, and in Jeremiah 44, written after the Babylonian captivity specifically to those Jews who had fled to Egypt! Both mention the idolatrous Queen of Heaven whom the Jewish women were worshiping.

Read Jeremiah 7:17–18, 28.

- What has happened in the streets of Jerusalem?

- What has perished in the streets of Jerusalem?

Read Jeremiah 7:30–34.

- What are they doing?

- What will be the consequences?

Read Jeremiah 42–44 for the context.

- What does Jeremiah 44:15 say the men realize?

- Why did the women go back to the practice of worshiping the Queen of Heaven?

- Why did the Lord say the calamity had come on them?

This was evidently a very old worship system that probably goes back to the Tower of Babel and the worship of the many false gods. The Queen of Heaven is possibly a name for the wife of Nimrod, the first world ruler who defied God. The idolatrous worship of the Queen of Heaven and her son Tammuz was carried into all cultures at the dispersal of humanity from the Tower of Babel. The Queen of Heaven has had many names throughout the ages in the cultures of all nations and is mentioned in their myths, but the teaching was the same. A woman miraculously giving birth to a son who is killed and resurrected is the basic myth of the Queen of Heaven. Babylon was the seedbed of the mother-child cult seen even in the Roman Catholic Church today.

Read Ezekiel 8:14. Who are the Jewish women weeping for at the Temple in Jerusalem? This is the blatant idolatry at God's house.

A Woman in a Basket Seen by Zechariah (520 BC)

Read Zechariah 5.

- What is this woman called?

- Where is she taken in the basket? Why?

Shinar is Babylon, associated with false gods and goddesses. Prostitution is a scriptural metaphor for unfaithfulness to the true God of heaven, Jehovah. False religion is sent by God back to its origin!

A Woman on a Beast Seen by John in Revelation (AD 95)

Read Revelation 17 and answer the following questions:

- What is she called, and where is she sitting in verses 1–2?

• With whom has she committed immorality?

• Where is she sitting in verse 3?

• What is her name in verse 5?

• What is her condition in verse 6?

• Why would she be associated with the Queen of Heaven?

Read Revelation 18:7–8 and compare with Isaiah 47:7–8. Does that help you answer the question above?

In Revelation 17:1–2, the woman is false religion, considering herself as indestructible, wealthy, powerful and in control of influencing the nations of the world. This false religion will form in the first half of the Tribulation, allowed by the beast and the ten kings to get unity.

Read Revelation 18:12–17.

- What is the attitude of the ten kings toward the woman in verse 15?

- What do they do with the help of the beast in verse 16?

- Who is really in control of this situation in verse 17?

This woman is called Mystery, Babylon the Great, the Mother of Harlots. The Tower of Babel is the source, or mother, of all false religions, especially the mother-child cult that taught the worship of the mother and her child—Satan's lie to detract from the true Son of God. However, Satan and his son, the Antichrist, and his government will turn on the false religion and destroy it in order to set up the ultimate false religious system, that of Satan worship and the worship of the Antichrist. There will be no atheism but the religion of the Antichrist claiming to be the way, the truth and the life—maybe even claiming to give eternal life through artificial intelligence or whatever big delusion he comes up with. He will claim to be God and demand worship or death!

> Europe is well-positioned as the new Babylon. They have kicked God out and invited Babylon in. They have exported satanic worship and a liberal lifestyle. They have promoted globalism, yet they are very anti-Israel. They fit the description remarkably well.
>
> *The Last Hour*, page 174

Application Truths from This Session

1. God calls His people out of Babylon in Revelation 18:4 and all through the New Testament. Any false religious system is a place of dwelling for the demons (see 18:2) and unclean spirits. Those cults who use the Bible and claim there is a mother in heaven and there is extra revelation added to the truth of the Bible are satanic, and true believers are to "come out of her."

2. The wealth and the influence of any false religion are only for a short time in the big scheme of eternity. Revelation 18:17 tells us who is really in control. Do you really trust God's Word completely? If so, can you give sound reasons why you trust the Word of God?

3. Our true citizenship is not on earth (see Philippians 3:20). This earth will become more and more anti-God as it becomes more difficult to live here and worship the one true God.

4. The good news is that the time is short. Satan's kingdom rule is not eternal, and Jesus will come to rule in righteousness and peace and to abolish all false religious systems (see Revelation 19).

5. God does not forget the sins of Babylon (see Revelation 18:4–6) and will make her pay doubly for them. However, God not only forgives the sins of believers, based on the blood of Jesus, but also has chosen to forget them! When you see the things in the book of Revelation that make you a bit anxious, just remember, you know the end of the story! How does that comfort you? Or does it?

6. In view of the enticement of Western society, do you sometimes find it difficult to "come out and be separate"? In what ways? Write it out and lay your struggles at the feet of Jesus, asking Him for strength to live righteously! He will honor that prayer!

11

DAYS OF EZEKIEL 36–37: WHAT WAS AND WHAT IS

These are the days of Ezekiel. We can see the prophecies of Ezekiel 36–39: those that have already taken place, those that are taking place at this present time and those that are about to take place. The return of the Jews to their home triggered this time of joy and tribulation.

The Last Hour, page 181

A s stated in the book, Ezekiel is a very unique prophet. His name means "God will strengthen." He was a priest of the Zadok family who was taken captive to Babylon with King Jehoiachin and other priestly families in 597 BC. He prophesied for about twenty years and was a contemporary of Jeremiah and Daniel. His life was completely under the appointment of God. Some have labeled him "the father of Judaism" because of his influence on the worship of Israel while in captivity away from Jerusalem and the Temple. Ezekiel's message is concerned first and foremost with the glory of the Lord, no matter what the vision was or how distant in the future the prophecies were.

Ezekiel was given messages emphasizing the sin of Jerusalem and Samaria (chapters 1–24); prophecies during Jerusalem's fall (chapters 25–32); and prophecies after Jerusalem's fall (chapters 33–48). The last section of prophecies given after Jerusalem's fall includes chapters 36–39, which speak of Israel's spiritual condition then and gives promises of the future for the nation. This book shows us a sovereign God in Israel who is over the affairs of the nations of the world. His sovereign will is that we should glorify Him in life and be a witness for Him to the ends of the earth. He wanted that for Israel in the Old Testament, and He wants that for the Church in the New Testament; however, as we also see in Ezekiel, God has a very specific plan for Israel, His chosen nation that was prophesied but is yet to be fulfilled. The fulfillment of Ezekiel 36–39 has begun but is not yet completely fulfilled. In this chapter we will look at the prophecies of Ezekiel 36–37, which are being fulfilled. In the following chapter, the prophecies of Ezekiel 38–39 that are still in the future will be studied.

Ezekiel 36: What Was—Restoration of the Land

Read the entire chapter of Ezekiel 36 in one sitting and then answer the following questions:

- What is Ezekiel specifically prophesying?

- What has happened to the mountains of Israel?

- Whose land is this? What have they endured?

- Who are the mountains of Israel called to bear fruit for and why?

- What are the promises in verses 10–12?

- What is the promise in verse 15?

- Why was the land under the judgment of God for almost two thousand years?

- What does God call the land?

- Have verses 26–27 been fulfilled?

- What does verse 30 prophesy?

- Why is God doing this?

Now that you have looked at the entire chapter, can you decide which verses have been fulfilled, at least since 1948? What examples of fulfillment does Amir give in the book on pages 181–184?

What promises are yet to be fulfilled?

History Lessons of Ezekiel 36

- Verses 1–7 describe the land of Israel taken over by the enemies of Israel. This happened in AD 70.
- Verses 8–15 describe a future time of fruitfulness from Ezekiel's time. That began in 1948, when Israel was reestablished as a nation, continuing even until today as they are more prosperous.
- Verses 16–21 chronicle God's longsuffering for His name throughout history.
- Verses 22–31 describe the national conversion of Israel. This is future—though they are a nation and are prosperous, they have yet to recognize that Jesus is their Messiah.
- Verses 32–38 make it very clear that God's glory is the sole object of the return of Israel and ultimately her conversion.

No other nation came into the land of Israel from AD 70 to 1948 and claimed Jerusalem as their capital, even though the Romans controlled the territory and then others, like the Byzantines. No one tilled the land or helped make it productive until God put it in the hearts of Jewish people to return to their land. It was because of the inquisitions and the pograms and ultimately the Holocaust that the people began to yearn for their own land. When the Jews began to trickle back into the land, they began to irrigate and work it, and God made it productive so that today they enjoy the land—but they still do not have the Spirit of God in their hearts and souls.

An important thing to remember is that there is a gap of time between the fruitfulness of the land and the spiritual conversion of the nation. They are in a fruitful, thriving land, but they do not believe in Jesus as a nation at this point.

Ezekiel 37—What Is the Resurrection of Dry Bones?

Read the entire chapter of Ezekiel 37 and answer the following questions.

- What is Ezekiel prophesying over (v. 4)?

- What miracle is pronounced (vv. 5–6)?

- What is happening in verses 7–8?

- What does Ezekiel prophesy to (v. 9)?

- What do the bones become (v. 10)?

- Who are the bones, and what do they say (v. 11)?

- What is God's promise (v. 12)?

- What is the land called (v. 12)?

- What will they know (v. 13)?

- What do they need for life?

- What are the promises to the scattered nation of Israel (vv. 15–22)?

- Where will the promises be fulfilled (v. 25)?

- What will God do, and why (v. 26)?

Doctrine of Ezekiel and Doctrine of Paul in Romans

- Forgiveness is necessary.
- Regeneration comes by the Spirit of God.
- The Spirit will indwell and rule the born-again.
- The national conversion of Israel as spoken of by Ezekiel and Paul in Romans 11—it is future!

Understanding the Vision of the Dry Bones of Israel

- Verses 1–10 speak of bones coming together with flesh and breath, a nation that became a vast army.
- Verses 11–14 explain that the bones represent the whole house of Israel, who felt they had no hope and were cut off as a nation—as seen in the metaphor of burial in the graves of the nations. They were a nation that seemed to be extinct, absorbed into the other nations of the world, yet God speaks and they literally come back into existence as a nation from the four corners of the earth. Only God gives life to a nation and individuals in nations. They have come back today as a nation, one nation, not a divided kingdom, but they are not a believing, forgiven, redeemed nation as described in Ezekiel 37.
- Verses 15–23 describe a united and converted nation.
- Verses 24–28 describe a Kingdom under a King. This is the Messianic Kingdom the Messiah will rule over for one thousand years when He returns to end all Gentile rule.

This prophecy covers the time Israel was scattered to the graveyards of the nations in AD 70 by the Gentile Roman Empire to 1948, when they came back to the land to become a nation, to the future God has for them in their millennial kingdom—united, restored, forgiven, redeemed under Jesus their Messiah. This prophecy is unlike any other prophecy ever given to any nation at any time!

Application Truths from This Session

1. The question we all must ask and answer—can dead bones live? The answer is only by the power of the Living God, who brings life through His Spirit to individuals and to a nation He has promised to restore. It is written—it will be accomplished!

2. We must all be born again, as Jesus told Nicodemus—born physically into this world, and born by the Spirit so we can live with Him eternally.

3. Read John 3, the entire chapter, and write out a prayer of thanksgiving if you are a believer, and one of confession of your sin and acceptance of Jesus as your Savior if you have never done so.

12

DAYS OF EZEKIEL 38-39: WHAT IS AND WHAT WILL BE

For the events of Ezekiel 38 to take place, the world needs to be either apathetic or hostile toward the nation of Israel. Currently, both aspects of that description most certainly apply. We also need to keep our eyes on Damascus, Syria. . . . Damascus will be leveled, a likely catalyst for the rest of the events of Ezekiel 38.

The Last Hour, page 189

The conflict we will look at in Ezekiel 38-39 is referred to by some as the war of Ezekiel. This is a war that has yet to occur, but will occur in the Middle East on the mountains of Israel when Israel is invaded by five nations that do not border her land but are a tier of nations beyond the borders of Israel. This war could be imminent today, but there are no time restrictions for this war except "the latter days."

We will examine what Ezekiel prophesied while in Babylon about these last days to see who enters the land of Israel, why they come and what the outcome is.

The Battle Begins—Ezekiel 38

Read Ezekiel 38 and answer the following questions:

- Who is the leader of this coalition (v. 3)?

- Who are the invading nations in (vv. 1, 5–6)?

- What time phrase do you see in verse 8?

- How do the invaders perceive this land to be (v. 11)?

- What do they covet (v. 12)?

- What nations question their actions (v. 13)?

- What is Ezekiel to prophesy to Gog (vv. 14–16)?

- What will God's response be to Gog (vv. 18–20)?

- God calls for a sword against Gog. Where will this occur (v. 21)?

- What does God use to defeat Gog (v. 22)?

- What will be the end result (v. 23)?

The Aftermath of the Invasion—Ezekiel 39

Read Ezekiel 39 and answer the following questions:

- Where does God say He has brought Gog from (vv. 1–2)?

- What does God have planned for Gog and his troops (vv. 3–5)?

- Why (v. 7)?

- Who will burn the weapons of war? For how long (vv. 9–10)?

- Where is Gog buried (v. 11)?

- How long does the burial of the dead take and why (vv. 12–13)?

- Who do the corpses provide a feast for (vv. 17–18)?

- God will get the glory from this war from two groups. Who are they (vv. 21–22)?

- What will the nations (Gentiles) learn about God's dealing with Israel (v. 23)?

- What are the promises to Israel (vv. 25–27)?

- What are the end results of this war (vv. 28–29)?

Summary of Ezekiel 38–39

Timing of the Ezekiel War

This war is prophesied to be in the "latter days." In Scripture, the latter days of the present age lead up to the "age to come," or the Messianic Age. This fits in with the days of the birthpangs of the Messiah in Matthew 24–25, leading up to the Tribulation of the last seven years, which will end "this age" and give way to the "age to come." There is a time frame mentioned in Ezekiel 39 referring to the burning of weapons for seven years; many place this war either right before the Tribulation or at the beginning of it. It will be a quick war, and this time frame will put the timing of the burning of weapons during the Tribulation.

Coalition of Nations of the Ezekiel War

A Russian-led coalition of Persia/Iran, Turkey, Libya and Sudan is described in Ezekiel 38–39. Today that exact coalition is in opposition to Israel and is positioned on the Syrian-Israeli border as this study is being written. They are predominantly Islamic nations except for Russia, who will use them because of their hatred for Israel.

Reason for the Invasion

Ezekiel 38:11–12 is very clear that they see those who have returned from their long exile in the nations as secure and prosperous, having "acquired goods" that they want to seize and plunder.

Outcome of the Invasion

Israel is protected by God; supernatural events like the coalition turning against each other, hail and an earthquake indicate God is in control! These are things Israel has no control over—only God can protect in this way. God has a zeal for His holy name and His land and His people. He wants the nations to know Him as well. He will do what it takes to get them to recognize Him as sovereign.

Application Truths from This Prophecy

1. God is in control even when leaders of nations plan and plot. God can overrule at any time.

2. God will accomplish His prophetic word and His will in His timing.

3. When Damascus is destroyed, it could be the spark that causes this explosive invasion of Israel.

4. America and Saudi Arabia and Europe are not in this war, and that is exactly where they stand at the present time—as onlookers but not there to get involved.

5. God is the only one Israel will have to depend on, not other nations—God alone. We, like Israel, need to learn this principle: We can never depend on the world to defend us as believers and take our side. If we are about God's will and His way, He will be our strength and our defense, and He alone will get the glory!

13

WHAT IS NEXT?

If you are looking for dates for what is coming next, you are going to be sorely disappointed. What we *can* know is the order of events. All we need to do is to look at the Bible and treat it as the literal Word of God. So many Christians get confused about what is next because they take random passages of Scripture and mix them. . . . The Bible was written as a whole. When we interpret it as a whole, rather than as random pieces of information, then the timeline begins to come into shape.

The Last Hour, pages 199–200

What are the next events on the timeline that the Bible says will happen before Jesus sets His feet on planet earth again? We will look at a few of those events in this last session together.

Events on the Timeline till Jesus Comes

What has occurred in the last century?

- The prophecies of Ezekiel 36–37. The physical land that is the same geographical land of Jesus two thousand years ago and of Abraham, Isaac and Jacob thirty-five hundred years before that has been restored, and the scattered Jews from the graveyards of the nations have returned. Israel is a recognized nation in the United Nations today.

- What has not yet occurred is the national salvation of Israel, when the nation of Israel recognizes their rejection of their true Messiah, Jesus, and asks Him to come and save them. This will occur at the end of the Tribulation—in their affliction, as Hosea 5:15 says.
- Psalm 83 lists a tier of nations that border Israel—Egypt, Jordan, Syria, Saudi Arabia. These nations wanted the annihilation of Israel as a nation so that "the name of Israel may be remembered no more" (v. 4). Those nations repeatedly attacked the nation of Holocaust survivors, but God stood on their side and they overcame. Today they are friendly with Egypt, Saudi Arabia and Jordan.
- The Suez Crisis (1956), the Six-Day War (1967), the War of Attrition (1967–70), the Yom Kippur War (1973) and the Lebanon Wars (1982, 2006) have all taken place.

What is in the future for an unbelieving world?

- Damascus will be destroyed—Isaiah 17:1.
- Israel will be invaded by the second tier of nations, which will be led by Russia—Ezekiel 38–39.
- A world government, led by ten kings, and a false world religion will rise—Daniel 7; Revelation 13.
- Revelation 6–9 will occur in the first half of the Tribulation, and the last half will be the terror reign of the Antichrist, who will get the power from seven of the ten kings/power brokers—today they might be seen as the elite who make decisions that will affect the entire world.
- The Jews in Judea will be forced to flee to Petra when the Antichrist declares himself God. God will protect them once again until they call on Him as a nation in their affliction—Hosea 5:15–6:2.

- Jesus will return to rescue the Jews from Bozrah, to save all Israel alive at that time and to judge the nations—Revelation 19; Zechariah 14.
- Jesus will set up the final millennial government and will rule and reign with His Bride, the Church, during that thousand-year period while Satan is bound—Revelation 20 and numerous Old Testament passages describe the millennial kingdom of Jesus.
- Then will come the final rebellion of Revelation 20 and the second resurrection of all the lost and the establishment of the new heaven and new earth for all eternity.

How then should we live as the Church until the Rapture occurs? How do we prepare ourselves for our Bridegroom, and how do we occupy till He comes?

All of the New Testament letters give the Church raw application for how to live in the last days. Here is a sampling of those exhortations

Read Romans 13:11–14. This is daily application for the Church until Jesus returns.

- It is now the hour "to awake out of _____; for now our salvation is _____ than when we first _____."
- "The night is far spent; the day is _____."
- We are to cast off works of _____ and put on the armor of _____.
- "Let us walk properly, as in the day, not in revelry and drunkenness, not in lewdness [sexual promiscuity] and lust, not in _____ and _____."
- "But put on the _____ _____, and make no provision for the _____, to fulfill its lusts."

Read 1 Thessalonians 5:11–22 for more practical application.

- "Therefore comfort each other and edify one another."
- "We urge you, brethren, to _____ those who labor among you, and are over you in the _____ and admonish

you, and to esteem them very highly in _____ for their work's sake."

- "Be at _____ among yourselves."
- "Warn those who are _____, comfort the _____; uphold the _____; be patient with _____."
- "See that no one renders _____ for _____ to anyone, but always pursue what is _____ both for yourselves and for _____."
- "In everything give _____; for this is the _____ of God in Christ Jesus for you."
- "Do not quench the _____. Do not despise _____. Test all things; hold _____ what is good. Abstain from every form of _____."

Read Colossians 2:8.

- "Beware lest anyone cheat you through _____ and empty _____, according to the _____ of men, according to the basic principles of the _____, and not according to Christ."

This is an important admonition to the Church, who can at times have "itching ears" and listen to the world and not have "ears to hear" from Jesus and His Word!

Read 1 Peter 5:8–10.

- "Be sober, be vigilant; because your adversary the _____ walks about like a roaring lion, seeking whom he may _____."
- "Resist him, steadfast in the _____, knowing that the same _____ are experienced by your brotherhood in the _____."
- "But may the God of all grace, who called us to His eternal glory by Christ Jesus, after you have suffered a _____, perfect, _____, _____, and settle you."

Application Truths to Remember in These Last Days

1. No one knows how long the Church will be here before the Lord returns. What we don't know either is how much persecution the Church will be allowed to go through.

2. We are not destined for the wrath of the Tribulation, but Peter told those believing Jews in the Diaspora and believers everywhere in the first century that Satan was out to devour whomever he could. That was and still is true. He said to hold fast to the faith and stand firm in the truths about God and His prophetic word, which they knew because His eyewitnesses, the apostles, had instructed them. He said the suffering was for a "little while," but we know the glory He has called us to is eternal.

3. We are to live out our time here as a faithful Bride looking for our Bridegroom, telling others He is coming and that they, too, can be part of the Bride if they only put their faith in Him, Jesus Christ of Nazareth!

4. Stay in His Word, which keeps you close to Him!

CLOSING WORDS OF AMIR

My goal in writing this book is not to cause fear but to bring peace. Fear comes from the unknown. Peace comes from understanding God's plan and seeing that He has things completely under control. I pray that as you finish this book, a hallelujah will be on your lips.

We are in the last hour. The countdown clock is nearing zero. While time winds down for the world, the hands on our clock are moving in the other direction. . . . If Jesus Christ is your Lord and Savior, you have eternal life. *Have* is a present tense verb, meaning you have it right now. Eternal life is not something you are waiting for; it is not something that you will receive when this life is over. Your eternal life is a reality as you are reading these words today. No matter what happens in the days you have left on earth, you have assurance of an eternal life with Christ.

The Last Hour, page 212

Believe in Him today if you have not done so already, and be blessed eternally!

May the God of peace Himself sanctify you completely; and may your whole spirit, soul, and body be preserved blameless at the coming of our Lord Jesus Christ. He who calls you is faithful, who also will do it.

1 Thessalonians 5:23–24

To Him be the glory and the dominion forever and ever. Amen!

1 Peter 5:11

Biblical Patterns and Foreshadowings
Timeline of God's Reversal

Timeline markers: ← Rapture (before Tribulation) · ← Second Coming (before Millennium) · ← Great White Throne (before Eternity)

	Creation	Fall	Flood	Babel	Abraham	Moses	Joshua	David	Exile/Return	Jesus	Church	Tribulation	Millennium	Eternity
Scripture	Gen. 1–2	Gen. 3–5	Gen. 6–9	Gen. 10–11	Gen 12–50	Ex.–Deut.				Matt.–John	Acts–Rev.	Rev. 6–20	Rev. 6–20	Rev. 21–22
Event			Remnant (8) left on earth to multiply and populate	Rebellion—did not scatter		Out of Egypt	Land	Covenant	Gentile powers control Jerusalem	Davidic covenant				New heaven / New earth / New Jerusalem
	No sin	Sin											Some sin	No sin
	No curse	Curse	Great Flood	United under Nimrod									Some death	No curse
	No death/pain	Death/pain	Destruction	Developed false religions										No death/pain
	No disasters	Danger	Spiritual depravity	Scattered nations and languages									No disasters	No disasters
	No disease	Crime	Violence	Violence/murder increases								Jacob's trouble—a time like no other		No disease
	No deformity	Violence	Violence											No deformity
	No temple	Thorns												No temple
	A Garden	Lost Garden	Longevity	Tower—Iraq (Rev. 17)										Tree of Life
	A River	Longevity	Life span decreases	Life span decreases									Longevity	River

First Coming Foreshadowed (Abraham–Moses)
- Isaac's miraculous birth → virgin birth
- Elijah & Elisha → Jesus' ministry, miracles, resurrection
- Passover lamb, offering Isaac → death of Jesus
- Sign of Jonah → resurrection of Jesus
- Moses' body not buried → ascension of Jesus

Second Coming Foreshadowed (Exile/Return–Church)
- Enoch & Elijah → Rapture
- Days of Noah, violence, plagues of Egypt, remnant → Tribulation
- Return to Babylon, rebuilt Temple → return to land in Millennium (partially restored 1948)
- Darkness and earthquakes at crucifixion → darkness and earthquakes in Egypt
- Noah's family left on earth to populate → Gentiles left on earth to populate in the Millennium

From Genesis to Revelation, God has consistently communicated with man to foreshadow and predict events that fulfill His plan of redemption through Jesus Christ. The timeline shows that what began in the Garden will end in the most glorious event called the Eternal Order. The parallels between the world at creation and then in eternity, between the fallen world and the millennial world, show a reversal of the evil and violence that characterize the period of time from the Flood to the Tribulation. The reversal will be complete when Jesus reigns for one thousand years and institutes the new heaven and the new earth.